math expressions

Common Core

Dr. Karen C. Fuson

Homework and Remembering Grade 6

Volume 1

This material is based upon work supported by the
National Science Foundation
under Grant Numbers
ESI-9816320, REC-9806020, and RED-935373.

Any opinions, findings, and conclusions, or recommendations expressed in this material
are those of the author and do not necessarily reflect the views of the National Science Foundation.

HMH

Copyright © by Houghton Mifflin Harcourt Publishing Company

All rights reserved. No part of this work may be reproduced or transmitted in any form or by any means, electronic or mechanical, including photocopying or recording, or by any information storage or retrieval system, without the prior written permission of the copyright owner unless such copying is expressly permitted by federal copyright law.

Permission is hereby granted to individuals using the corresponding student's textbook or kit as the major vehicle for regular classroom instruction to photocopy copying masters from this publication in classroom quantities for instructional use and not for resale. Requests for information on other matters regarding duplication of this work should be submitted through our Permissions website at https://customercare.hmhco.com/contactus/Permissions.html or mailed to Houghton Mifflin Harcourt Publishing Company, Attn: Intellectual Property Licensing, 9400 Southpark Center Loop, Orlando, Florida 32819-8647.

Printed in the U.S.A.

ISBN 978-1-328-70272-2

2 3 4 5 6 7 8 9 10 0982 26 25 24 23 22 21 20 19 18 17

4500662086   B C D E F G

If you have received these materials as examination copies free of charge, Houghton Mifflin Harcourt Publishing Company retains title to the materials and they may not be resold. Resale of examination copies is strictly prohibited.

Possession of this publication in print format does not entitle users to convert this publication, or any portion of it, into electronic format.

1-1 Homework   Name _____   Date _____

① Complete the Multiplication Table.

•		2		4	5		7	8	9
1	1	2	3		5	6		8	9
	2	4		8		12	14		18
3			9		15	18		24	
	4	8		16		24	28		36
5	5	10	15		25		35		45
			18	24	30	36		48	
7		14						56	
	8			32	40		56		72
9	9	18	27		45	54		72	

② Complete the Scrambled Multiplication Table.

•		5		4		3		2	6
4		20		36		12			24
1			8		9	7		1	
8		64	32		56	24		16	
		15			21		3	6	
7		35		28	63		21	14	42
		25		20		35		5	10
6		30	48		54		18	6	36
9			72	36	81		27	9	18
		10		8		14	6	2	12

③ Describe your strategy for filling in the top row of the Scrambled Multiplication Table.

_____

_____

UNIT 1 LESSON 1   Factor Puzzles and the Multiplication Table 1

1-1 Remembering

Multiply or divide.

1. $42 \div 6 =$ _____
2. _____ $= 56 \div 7$
3. _____ $= 8 \times 9$
4. _____ $= 7 \times 4$
5. $9 \cdot 4 =$ _____
6. _____ $= \frac{63}{7}$
7. $6 \cdot 6 =$ _____
8. _____ $= 6 \cdot 9$
9. $81 \div 9 =$ _____
10. $\frac{72}{9} =$ _____
11. _____ $= 8 \times 4$
12. _____ $= 48 \div 8$
13. _____ $= 8 \cdot 8$
14. $24 \div 6 =$ _____
15. _____ $= \frac{36}{6}$

Represent the situation with an equation. Solve.

16. The town planted 3 new trees in the park. Now there are 27 trees. How many trees were there before the new trees were planted?

    Equation: _____

    Answer: _____

17. In the school parking lot, there are 6 rows of cars with 30 cars in each row. How many cars are there in the school parking lot?

    Equation: _____

    Answer: _____

18. At the start of the day on Friday, 40 tickets had been sold to the school play. During the day, some more tickets were sold. By the end of the day on Friday, 48 tickets were sold. How many tickets were sold during the day on Friday?

    Equation: _____

    Answer: _____

19. Arun has 3 birds. He has 6 times as many goldfish as birds. How many goldfish does Arun have?

    G | 3 | 3 | 3 | 3 | 3 | 3 |
    B | 3 |

    Equation: _____

    Answer: _____

20. **Stretch Your Thinking** Cary bought a large bag of 12 apples and 3 small bags with 6 apples each. How many apples did Cary buy? Hint: Use parentheses if you need to.

    Equation: _____

    Answer: _____

1-2 Homework

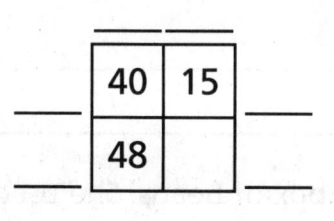

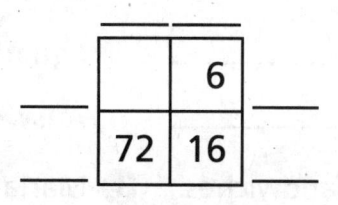

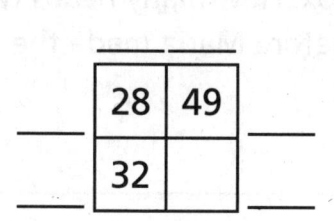

Solve each Factor Puzzle.

1.
12	15
8	

2.
8	
14	21

3.
8	12
	15

4.
15	35
18	

5.
32	40
	45

6.
	24
35	42

7.
40	15
48	

8.
	6
72	16

9.
63	27
35	

10.
28	49
32	

11.
63	72
28	

12.
49	
42	24

13. Describe strategies for solving a Factor Puzzle.

_____

_____

UNIT 1 LESSON 2   Solving Factor Puzzles **3**

1-2 Remembering

Multiply or divide.

1. _____ = 9 × 7
2. 36 ÷ 6 = _____
3. _____ = 48 ÷ 8
4. _____ = $\frac{56}{8}$
5. _____ = 7 × 7
6. 8 · 7 = _____
7. 81 ÷ 9 = _____
8. 4 · 7 = _____
9. _____ = 8 · 8
10. _____ = $\frac{32}{8}$
11. 6 · 8 = _____
12. _____ = $\frac{16}{4}$
13. _____ = 54 ÷ 6
14. $\frac{72}{9}$ = _____
15. _____ = 6 × 7

Represent the situation with an equation. Solve.

16. Vincent had 120 baseball cards. Then he bought some more. Now he has 160 cards. How many cards did Vincent buy?

    Equation: _____

    Answer: _____

17. Frank buys 8 packages of light bulbs. There are 4 light bulbs in each package. How many light bulbs does he buy?

    Equation: _____

    Answer: _____

18. Mrs. Martin made 12 tuna sandwiches. This was 3 times the number of cheese sandwiches that she made. How many cheese sandwiches did she make?

T	4	4	4
C	4		

    Equation: _____

    Answer: _____

19. Maria has a box of beads. She used 60 beads to make a necklace for her mother. Now there are 420 beads left in the box. How many beads were in the box before Maria made the necklace?

    Equation: _____

    Answer: _____

20. **Stretch Your Thinking** Jared ran 7 miles on Monday and 3 times as far on Tuesday. How many more miles did Jared run on Tuesday than on Monday? Hint: Use parentheses if you need to.

    Equation: _____

    Answer: _____

Solving Factor Puzzles

1-3 Homework

Complete this story about Noreen's older brother, Tim.

Tim saved $5 every day. Noreen and Tim both started to save on the same day. Draw pictures of Tim's bank each day if that helps you decide how much he has saved.

Tim began with an empty coin bank.

1. On Day 1 Tim put $5 into his coin bank.

   On Day 1 Tim had _____ in his bank.

2. On Day 2 Tim put $5 into his coin bank.

   On Day 2 Tim had _____ in his bank.

3. On Day 3 Tim put $5 into his coin bank.

   On Day 3 Tim had _____ in his bank.

4. On Day 4 Tim put $5 into his coin bank.

   On Day 4 Tim had _____ in his bank.

5. On Day 5 Tim put $5 into his coin bank.

   On Day 5 Tim had _____ in his bank.

6. On Day 6 Tim put $5 into his coin bank.

   On Day 6 Tim had _____ in his bank.

7. On Day 7 Tim put $5 into his coin bank.

   On Day 7 Tim had _____ in his bank.

8. On Day 8 Tim put $5 into his coin bank.

   On Day 8 Tim had _____ in his bank.

9. Complete the rate table to show Tim's savings.

Days	Dollars
1	
2	
3	
4	
5	
6	
7	
8	

UNIT 1 LESSON 3 — Rate Situations and Rate Tables 5

1-3 Remembering

Multiply or divide.

1. $56 \div 7 =$ _____
2. _____ $= 72 \div 8$
3. _____ $= 9 \cdot 9$
4. $8 \cdot 4 =$ _____
5. _____ $= 7 \cdot 6$
6. $56 \div 8 =$ _____
7. _____ $= 6 \cdot 4$
8. $36 \div 6 =$ _____
9. _____ $= \frac{28}{7}$
10. $7 \cdot 7 =$ _____
11. _____ $= \frac{16}{4}$
12. _____ $= \frac{63}{7}$
13. $\frac{32}{8} =$ _____
14. _____ $= 7 \cdot 4$
15. _____ $= 64 \div 8$

Represent the situation with an equation. Solve.

16. Marcie plants 42 tomato plants in 6 equal rows. How many plants are in each row?

    Equation: _____

    Answer: _____

17. There are 12 slices of toast on a tray. Roberto takes 2 slices. How many slices are on the tray now?

    Equation: _____

    Answer: _____

18. There are 240 fewer teachers than students at Westside Middle School. There are 10 teachers. How many students are there?

    Equation: _____

    Answer: _____

19. Al practiced the piano 10 hours this week and 5 hours last week. How many times as many hours did Al practice the piano this week than last week?

    Equation: _____

    Answer: _____

20. **Stretch Your Thinking** Mrs. Ortiz bought a tablecloth for $5 and 6 napkins for $2 each. What was the total cost?

    Hint: Use parentheses if you need to.

    Equation: _____

    Answer: _____

6 UNIT 1 LESSON 3   Rate Situations and Rate Tables

1-4 Homework

For each situation, decide whether there is a constant rate. If *yes*, write the rate and complete the rate table.

1. Grandma Jackson has 5 plants in each row in her garden.

Is there a constant rate? _____

_____ _____ per _____

Unit	Product
1	
2	
3	

2. A large bag of potatoes costs $8 at Season's Produce Store.

Is there a constant rate? _____

_____ _____ per _____

Unit	Product
1	
2	
3	

3. Write a story for this rate table. Label the columns to tell your story.

_____
_____
_____
_____

Unit	Product
1	7
2	14
3	21
4	28
5	35
6	42
7	49

Solve each Factor Puzzle.

4.

15	21
40	

5.

10	
18	63

6.

35	15
	18

UNIT 1 LESSON 4 — Rate Situations and Unit Rate Language **7**

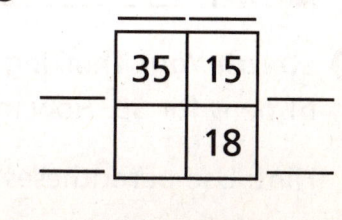

1-4 Remembering

Complete each Factor Puzzle.

1.
```
___  ___
| 10 | 8 |
| 15 |   |
___  ___
```

2.
```
___  ___
|    | 8 |
| 15 | 20|
___  ___
```

3.
```
___  ___
| 8  | 18|
|    | 63|
___  ___
```

4.
```
___  ___
| 8  | 14|
| 36 |   |
___  ___
```

5.
```
___  ___
| 24 |   |
| 28 | 63|
___  ___
```

6.
```
___  ___
|    | 18|
| 35 | 42|
___  ___
```

Represent the situation with an equation. Solve.

7. If Maria places 40 roses equally into 5 vases, how many roses will she put in each vase?

Equation: _____

Answer: _____

8. Ben scored 24 points. Vince scored 8 points. How many fewer points did Vince score than Ben?

Equation: _____

Answer: _____

9. The school library has 400 fiction books. Fifty are paperback and the rest are hardcover. How many of the fiction books are hardcover?

Equation: _____

Answer: _____

10. Julie buys shoes and a shirt. The shoes cost 5 times as much as the shirt. The shirt cost $6. How much do the shoes cost?

Equation: _____

Answer: _____

11. Stretch Your Thinking Jake bought a notebook for $2 and a package of pens for $5. How much change did he get back from $10?

Hint: Use parentheses if you need to.

Equation: _____

Answer: _____

8 UNIT 1 LESSON 4 — Rate Situations and Unit Rate Language

1-5 Homework

For each rate situation, find the unit rate and write it using *per*. Make a rate table that includes the given information as the first row in the table. Continue making a scrambled rate table.

1 Aunt Suzy's rectangular garden has 40 carrot plants in the first 8 rows.

_____ _____ per _____

Unit	Product
___	___
1	
	25
	15

2 Each week Aki eats the same number of oranges. In 7 weeks, she ate 28 oranges.

_____ _____ per _____

Unit	Product
___	___
1	
4	
	8

3 Every week Noreen eats half a dozen oranges.

_____ _____ per _____

Unit	Product
___	___

4 In the spring, David plants 8 tomato plants in each row of his garden.

_____ _____ per _____

Unit	Product
___	___

5 Jason saves $4 every day so that he can buy a basketball hoop.

_____ _____ per _____

Unit	Product
___	___

6 Carole feeds her tropical fish 6 pinches of food every day.

_____ _____ per _____

Unit	Product
___	___

1-5 Remembering

Complete each Factor Puzzle.

1.
	15
27	72

2.
	45
24	54

3.
24	28
	30

4.
14	63
	27

5.
48	
54	63

6.
56	32
	28

Represent the situation with an equation. Solve.

7. In a parking lot, there are 6 rows of cars with 30 cars parked in each row. How many cars are in the lot?

   Equation: _____

   Answer: _____

8. Andrew jogged 24 miles today. This is 2 times as far as he jogged yesterday. How far did he jog yesterday?

   Equation: _____

   Answer: _____

9. The cafeteria sold 30 more oranges than apples. The cafeteria sold 270 oranges. How many apples did they sell?

   Equation: _____

   Answer: _____

10. Ed has 18 red goldfish. He has 6 times as many red goldfish as orange goldfish. How many orange goldfish does he have?

    Equation: _____

    Answer: _____

11. **Stretch Your Thinking** There are 3 stacks with 8 books each and 4 stacks with 9 books each. How many books are there in all?

    Hint: Use parentheses if you need to.

    Equation: _____

    Answer: _____

1-6 Homework

For each table, find the unit price. Then complete the table.

1) At Best Buy Fruits, 9 boxes of strawberries cost $36. What is the unit price for 1 box? _____

Number of Boxes	Cost in Dollars
1	
9	36
5	
	28
	32
100	

2) At Yummy Fruits, 6 boxes of strawberries cost $42. What is the unit price for 1 box? _____

Number of Boxes	Cost in Dollars
1	
6	42
10	
	21
	63
	14

3) **a.** For Exercises 1 and 2, what assumption did you have to make for these to be constant rate situations?
_____

b. Is your assumption reasonable?
_____

c. Describe a situation when the strawberries at Yummy Fruits might be a better buy than the strawberries at Best Buy Fruits.
_____
_____

d. The graph shows the three lines you graphed in this lesson. Each line shows the cost for a different kind of granola.
Describe where the line for the cost of strawberries at Best Buy Fruits and the line for the cost of strawberries at Yummy Fruits would go on this graph.

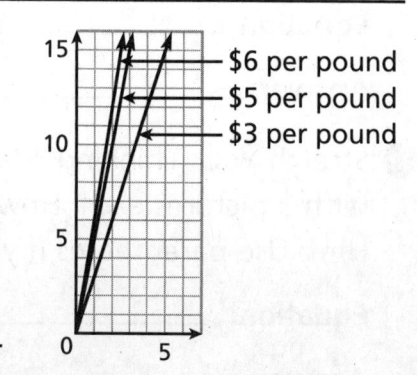

— $6 per pound
— $5 per pound
— $3 per pound

_____

UNIT 1 LESSON 6 — Unit Pricing 11

1-6 Remembering

Complete each Factor Puzzle.

1.
12	8
15	

2.
	10
12	15

3.
12	
27	63

4.
8	
28	63

5.
28	32
	72

6.
	36
56	63

Represent the situation with an equation. Solve.

7. A store had 360 bottles of water. Some of the bottles were sold. Then there were 150 bottles of water. How many bottles were sold?

Equation: _____

Answer: _____

8. There are 150 girls and 140 boys signed up for the after-school science club. How many students are signed up for the science club?

Equation: _____

Answer: _____

9. A florist sold 4 fewer tulips than roses. The florist sold 80 roses. How many tulips did the florist sell?

Equation: _____

Answer: _____

10. Matt's string is 15 inches long. Sabrina's string is 3 times as long as Matt's. How long is Sabrina's string?

Equation: _____

Answer: _____

11. Stretch Your Thinking Mario has 9 pictures to hang. He hangs 2 rows with 3 pictures each. How many pictures does he have left to hang? Hint: Use parentheses if you need to.

Equation: _____

Answer: _____

1-7 Homework

1. Circle the unit rate in the table. Use the unit rate to complete the table. Draw the graph and show the unit rate triangle.

Time	Distance
Seconds	Yards
1	6
	18
	24
2	

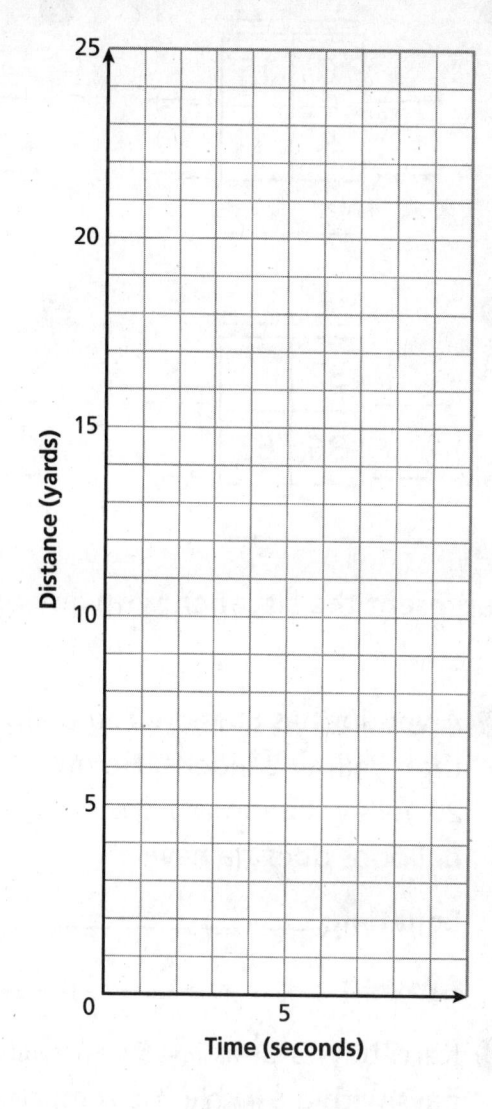

These rate tables show the speed of three different runners. Fill in the missing values in each table.

2.

Time	Distance
Seconds	Yards
1	2
	4
3	
	8
5	

3.

Time	Distance
Seconds	Yards
1	
2	
	25
8	
10	50

4.

Time	Distance
Seconds	Yards
	24
1	
4	12
2	
	15

UNIT 1 LESSON 7   Constant Speed **13**

1-7 Remembering

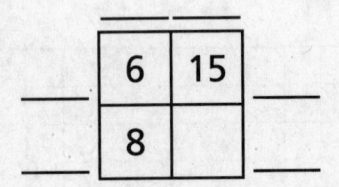

Complete each Factor Puzzle.

1.
6	15
8	

2.
	6
20	15

3.
	6
16	56

4.
32	
36	63

5.
6	16
	56

6.
	63
32	72

Represent the situation with an equation. Solve.

7. A vendor has 80 more red balloons than yellow balloons. He has 20 yellow balloons. How many red balloons does he have?

Equation: _____

Answer: _____

8. Sam works in a bakery. If he has 54 bagels and he puts 6 bagels in each bag, how many bags does he use?

Equation: _____

Answer: _____

9. Kerri buys 3 pens for $1.50 each. She pays with a $10 bill. How much change should she get back?

Equation: _____

Answer: _____

10. A theater has 10 rows of seats with 8 seats in each row. If 28 people are seated, how many seats are empty?

Equation: _____

Answer: _____

11. Stretch Your Thinking A room has 9 tables with 6 chairs each and 7 tables with 8 chairs each. How many chairs are in the room altogether? Hint: Use parentheses if you need to.

Equation: _____

Answer: _____

14 UNIT 1 LESSON 7 — Constant Speed

1-8 Homework

Noreen and Tim plant carrots in their garden. They each plant rows at the same time. Noreen plants 4 carrot seeds in each row. Tim plants 9 carrot seeds in each row.

Rows	N 4	T 9
1	4	9
2	8	18
3	12	27
4	16	36
5	20	45
6	24	54
7	28	63

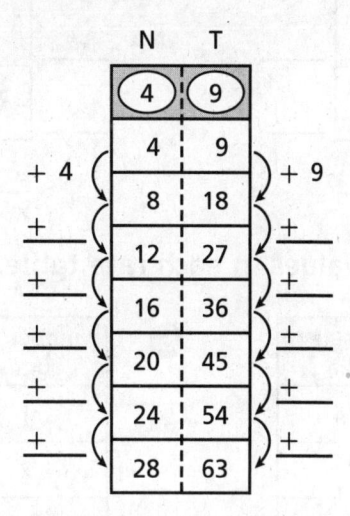

	N 4	T 9	
+ 4	4	9	+ 9
+ __	8	18	+ __
+ __	12	27	+ __
+ __	16	36	+ __
+ __	20	45	+ __
+ __	24	54	+ __
+ __	28	63	+ __

1 How are the tables alike? How are they different?

_____

_____

_____

2 What are the numbers circled at the top of each table? _____

3 Fill in the numbers to the left and right of the ratio table to show Noreen's and Tim's constant increases.

Use the tables to answer each question.

4 Noreen has planted 12 carrot seeds. How many has Tim planted?

_____ carrot seeds

How many rows is this? _____ rows

5 Tim has planted 63 carrot seeds. How many has Noreen planted?

_____ carrot seeds

How many rows is this? _____ rows

UNIT 1 LESSON 8   Ratio as Linked Rates **15**

1-8 Remembering

Complete each Factor Puzzle.

1.
	15	35
		63

2.
		27
	32	24

3.
	40	35
		32

Fill in the missing values in each rate table.

4.
Number of Pounds	Cost in Dollars
1	4
2	
3	
	16
5	
	24

5.
Number of Pounds	Cost in Dollars
1	7
2	
	28
	35
10	
	700

6.
Number of Pounds	Cost in Dollars
1	
8	
	18
6	54
	180
	36

Represent the situation with an equation. Solve. Use parentheses if you need to.

7. Bob's Bakery sold 10 bags of bagels containing a dozen bagels each and 30 bags of bagels containing a half dozen each. How many bagels did the bakery sell in all?

Equation: _____

Answer: _____

8. Stretch Your Thinking Brendan lives 2 miles closer to the library than Jamal does. Jamal lives 1 mile farther from the library than Aisha does. Jamal lives 3 miles from the library. How much closer to the library is Brendan than Aisha?

Equation: _____

Answer: _____

1-9 Homework

Name _____ Date _____

Make a ratio table for each situation. Be sure to label the columns.

① Noreen and Tim each plant groups of flowers in their gardens. Noreen plants 3 in a group while Tim plants 5 in a group.

② Grammy Suzy's recipe for summer salad is 2 cucumbers for every 3 tomatoes.

③ Royal purple paint color is made from 3 cans of red paint and 7 cans of blue paint.

Ratio Table 1

The linking unit is _____.

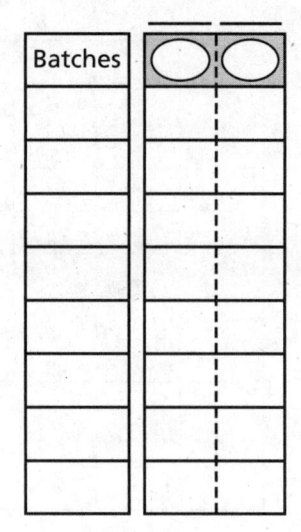

Ratio Table 2

Batches

The linking unit is _____.

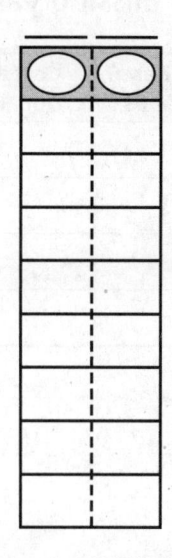

Ratio Table 3

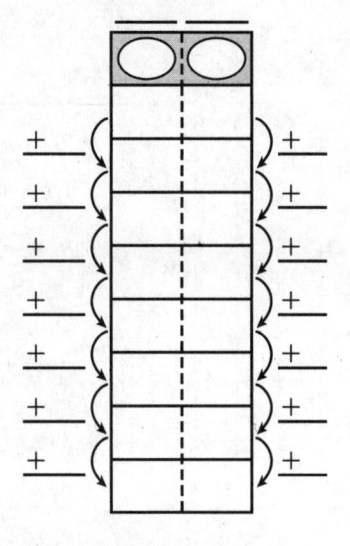

The linking unit is _____.

④ Circle each ratio table below. Write numbers to show the two multiplication columns that are in each ratio table.

A.

7	3
14	6
21	9
28	12
35	15
42	18
49	21

B.

2	3
4	5
6	8
8	10
10	13
12	15
14	18

C.

9	4
18	8
27	12
36	16
45	20
54	24
63	28

D.

1	1
1	2
1	3
1	4
1	5
1	6
1	7

UNIT 1 LESSON 9   Finding Linked Values in Ratio Tables

1-9 Remembering

Complete each Factor Puzzle.

1)
10	12
	42

2)
	18
40	15

3)
36	63
32	

Fill in the missing values in the rate table. Draw the graph.

4)
Number of Pounds	Cost in Dollars
1	
2	
3	6
	8

Represent the situation with an equation. Solve.
Use parentheses if you need to.

5) Section A in a stadium has 30 rows of seats with 20 seats in each row. Section B has 4 times as many seats as Section A. How many seats are in Section B?

Equation: _____

Answer: _____

6) **Stretch Your Thinking** A balloon vendor sold 225 balloons on Saturday. He sold red, yellow, and blue balloons. He sold 100 red balloons and 25 more red than blue. How many yellow balloons did he sell?

Equation: _____

Answer: _____

18 UNIT 1 LESSON 9   Finding Linked Values in Ratio Tables

1-10 Homework

Use Factor Puzzles to solve these proportion problems.

Diana and Walter are twins who both do these activities for the same amount of time but at their own constant rates.

① a. Diana read 15 pages and Walter read 35 pages. How many pages had Diana read when Walter had read 14 pages?

_____ pages

b. Fill in the ratio table and circle the rows that make the Factor Puzzle.

② Diana sold 35 tickets and Walter sold 56 tickets. How many tickets had Walter sold when Diana had sold 15 tickets?

_____ tickets

③ Diana sliced 24 bananas while Walter sliced 16 bananas. When Diana had sliced 21 bananas, how many bananas had Walter sliced?

_____ bananas

④ Walter drew 6 pictures while Diana drew 8 pictures. When Diana had drawn 28 pictures, how many had Walter drawn?

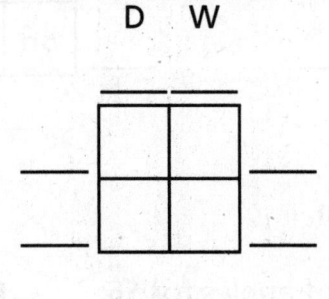

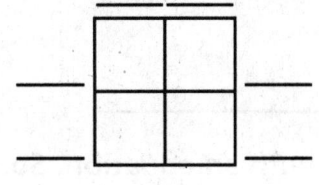

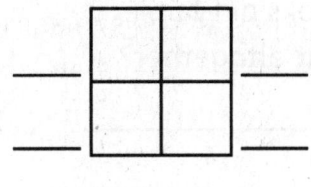

_____ pictures

UNIT 1 LESSON 10   Seeing Proportions in Ratio Tables **19**

1-10 Remembering

Complete each Factor Puzzle.

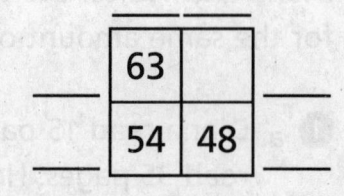

①
40	32
35	

②
	72
36	81

③
63	
54	48

Solve each rate problem.

④ Sam buys 3 pounds of apples for $6. What is the unit rate?

⑤ Ashley earns $5 per hour babysitting. How much will she earn in 3 hours?

⑥ Marcus walks 9 miles in 3 hours. What is his unit rate?

⑦ Mrs. Dunn drives at a constant rate of 55 miles per hour for 2 hours. How far does she drive?

Represent the situation with an equation. Solve. Use parentheses if you need to.

⑧ Jamie took out 4 books from the library. His sister took out 3 times as many. How many books did Jamie and his sister take out altogether?

Equation: _____

Answer: _____

⑨ There are 9 red apples in a bowl. There are 4 fewer green apples than red apples. How many apples are in the bowl?

Equation: _____

Answer: _____

⑩ **Stretch Your Thinking** In a video game, Lee scored 500 points. Andrew scored twice as many points as Lee. Ed scored 100 more points than Lee. How many more points did Andrew score than Ed?

Equation: _____

Answer: _____

20 UNIT 1 LESSON 10　　Seeing Proportions in Ratio Tables

1-11 Homework

Tell why the situation is a proportion or write the assumption that must be stated to make the problem a proportion problem.

Use a Factor Puzzle to solve the problem.

1 To make a pale blue paint, Erica mixes 6 cans of blue and 10 cans of white. She has 35 cans of white paint. How many cans of blue does she need to get the same pale blue?

____ cans

2 Friendly Florist sells bunches with 16 daisies and 6 roses. Aunt Lynn wants a large bunch in the same ratio. If she gets 40 daisies, how many roses will she get?

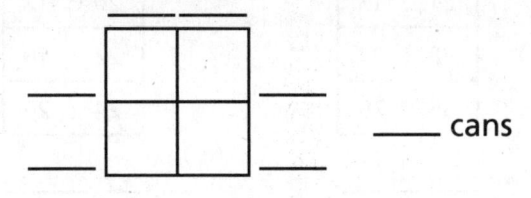

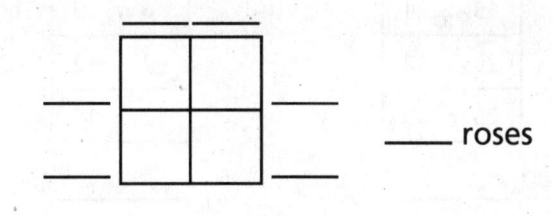

____ roses

3 Central School has 6 printers and 14 computers. If East School has 28 computers, how many printers does it have?

____ printers

4 The twins baked pancakes using 10 cups of mix and 15 eggs. Everyone wants more, but they only have 12 eggs left. How many cups of mix should they use?

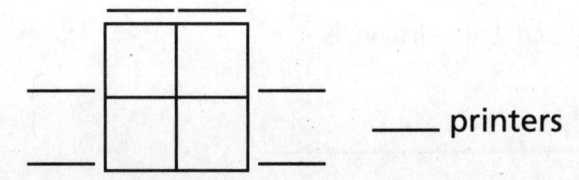

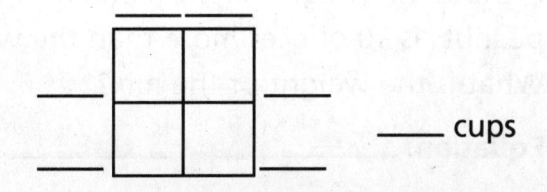

____ cups

UNIT 1 LESSON 11 — Identify and Solve Proportional Situations

1-11 Remembering

Complete each Factor Puzzle.

1
15	24
	56

2
	63
56	72

3
56	
63	54

Is the table a ratio table? Write *yes* or *no*.
If *yes*, write the basic ratio at the top of the table.

4
◯ : ◯
5 : 8
10 : 16
15 : 24
20 : 32
25 : 40

_____

5
◯ : ◯
2 : 3
4 : 6
6 : 9
7 : 12
12 : 15

_____

6
◯ : ◯
7 : 5
14 : 10
21 : 15
28 : 20
35 : 25

_____

7
◯ : ◯
6 : 4
12 : 8
20 : 12
22 : 16
24 : 20

_____

Represent the situation with an equation. Solve.
Use parentheses if you need to.

8 The book Maria is reading has 50 pages. Her sister Abigail's book has 3 times as many pages. How many more pages are in Abigail's book than in Maria's book?

Equation: _____

Answer: _____

9 Stretch Your Thinking A nut mix contains three kinds of nuts. There are 5 ounces of almonds. The weight of the cashews is triple the weight of the almonds and the weight of the peanuts is 10 ounces more than the weight of the almonds. What is the weight of the mix?

Equation: _____

Answer: _____

Identify and Solve Proportional Situations

1-12 Homework

Name _____ Date _____

Show the Factor Puzzle for each proportion. Solve.

① 18:54 = c:42

c = _____

② 27:63::12:q

q = _____

③ 12:50 = a:75

a = _____

Dear Math Students,

Today I was mixing blue paint and red paint to make purple paint. I mixed 14 cups of blue with 42 cups of red and I got a really nice purple color. I needed more paint. I had 12 more cups of red, so I used this Factor Puzzle to find out how much blue I should mix in. I got my answer, 36 cups.

So, I mixed in 36 cups of blue with the 12 cups of red and the purple color was not the same as the first batch.

Did I do something wrong? Can you help?

Your friend,
Puzzled Penguin

B	R
14	42
12	

④ Write a response to Puzzled Penguin.

_____
_____
_____
_____

UNIT 1 LESSON 12 — Solve Numeric Proportion Problems

1-12 Remembering

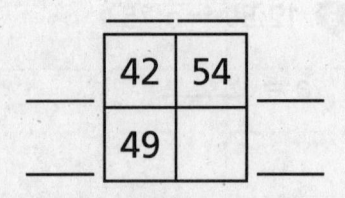

Complete each Factor Puzzle.

1
	42	54
	49	

2
		6
	4	3

3
	20	
	36	63

Circle each ratio table below. Write numbers to show the two multiplication columns that are in each ratio table.

4 ◯ : ◯
5	:	7
10	:	14
15	:	28
20	:	35
25	:	42
30	:	49
35	:	63

5 ◯ : ◯
3	:	7
6	:	14
9	:	21
12	:	28
15	:	35
18	:	42
21	:	49

6 ◯ : ◯
3	:	4
3	:	8
3	:	12
3	:	16
3	:	20
3	:	24
3	:	28

7 ◯ : ◯
2	:	5
4	:	10
6	:	15
8	:	20
10	:	25
12	:	30
14	:	35

Represent the situation with an equation. Solve.
Use parentheses if you need to.

8 Marna's display has 3 rows of stamps with 9 stamps in each row. Ned's display has 1 fewer row but 2 more stamps in each row. How many stamps are in Ned's display?

Equation: _____

Answer: _____

9 **Stretch Your Thinking** A fruit basket has 6 apples. It has twice as many oranges as apples and twice as many apples as bananas. How many more oranges than bananas are there?

Equation: _____

Answer: _____

24 UNIT 1 LESSON 12

Solve Numeric Proportion Problems

1-13 Homework

Name _____ **Date** _____

1 Write a word problem for the proportion 6:15 = n:35.

_____
_____
_____
_____

Solve.

2 4:7 :: m:42

m = _____

3 3:d :: 27:45

d = _____

4 What is the basic ratio for 12:27?

_____

5 The basic ratio for 120:150 is _____.

6 The basic ratio for 24:56 is _____.

7 Danny fills each vase with 5 roses and 9 irises. How many irises will he use if he uses 30 roses?

_____

8 Dede's cost ratio for large balloons to small balloons was $15 to $6. Her sister Fran's ratio was ■ to $14. How much did Fran pay for her large balloons?

_____

UNIT 1 LESSON 13

Basic Ratio Solution Strategies **25**

1-13 Remembering

Complete each Factor Puzzle.

1.

7	2
56	

2.

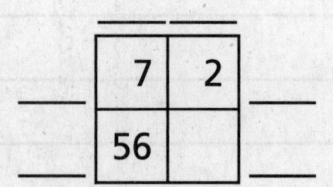

36	32
	72

3.

72	
8	7

Complete each ratio table. Write the basic ratio.

4. ◯ : ◯

12	:
36	: 63
	: 14
28	:
16	:
	: 42
	: 35

5. ◯ : ◯

	: 35
	: 40
9	:
18	:
6	: 10
	: 25
12	:

6. ◯ : ◯

4	:
8	:
	: 9
14	: 21
	: 18
16	:
10	:

7. ◯ : ◯

	: 14
8	:
	: 42
	: 28
40	:
56	:
24	: 21

Represent the situation with an equation. Solve. Use parentheses if you need to.

8. Andy picked 5 tulips. Brianna picked 3 more tulips than Andy. Carley picked 16 tulips. How many times as many tulips did Carley pick than Brianna?

Equation: _____

Answer: _____

9. Stretch Your Thinking Mrs. Martinez bakes 5 pans of cornbread and cuts each pan of cornbread so that there are 3 rows with 4 pieces in each row. How many more pieces could she have gotten if she had cut each pan of cornbread so that there were 4 rows with 5 pieces in each row?

Equation: _____

Answer: _____

1-14 Homework

Circle the number of the problem that is not a proportion problem. Solve each proportion problem.

1 3:5 :: 21:r

r = _____

2 b:7 :: 16:56

b = _____

3 What is the basic ratio for 30:42?

_____

4 The basic ratio for 36:84 is _____.

5 What is the basic ratio for 5:15? _____

6 In the zoo, there are 6 flamingos for every 8 ducks. If there are 20 ducks, how many flamingos are there?

_____

7 Josh and Sally each bike at their own constant rates. Josh bikes 35 miles while Sally bikes 40 miles. If Sally bikes 16 miles, how far does Josh bike?

_____

8 Alice is delivering mail on Maple Street. She has letters for house #4 and #6. If she has letters for #20, what other house does she have letters for?

_____

9 9:24 :: 24:d

d = _____

UNIT 1 LESSON 14 — Write and Solve Proportion Problems 27

1-14 Remembering

Complete each Factor Puzzle.

①
20	45
	63

②
	12
35	10

③
6	
48	56

Show the Factor Puzzle for each proportion. Solve.

④ $a:18 = 35:45$

⑤ $15:12 = b:28$

⑥ $15:c = 5:2$

$a = $ _____

$b = $ _____

$c = $ _____

Represent the situation with an equation. Solve. Use parentheses if you need to.

⑦ Yesterday a bakery made 360 bagels. They packed them in bags of 6. They sold 45 bags. How many bags were left?

Equation: _____

Answer: _____

⑧ Al scored 250 points. This was 25 points more than Ben. Kim scored twice as many points as Ben. What was Kim's score?

Equation: _____

Answer: _____

⑨ **Stretch Your Thinking** On Wednesday, Felipe drove 150 miles. This was 3 times the distance he drove on Monday and 40 miles more than he drove on Tuesday. How many miles did Felipe drive in the three days?

Equation: _____

Answer: _____

28 UNIT 1 LESSON 14

1-15 Homework

Use your reasoning skills to develop a set of data that will graph as a line. Write your data in the table below, and then plot the ordered pairs to verify that the data plot in a line.

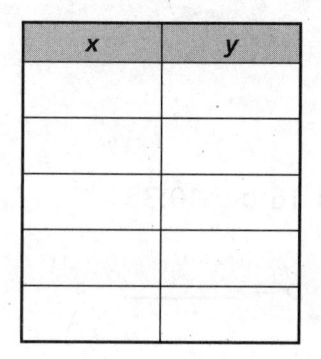

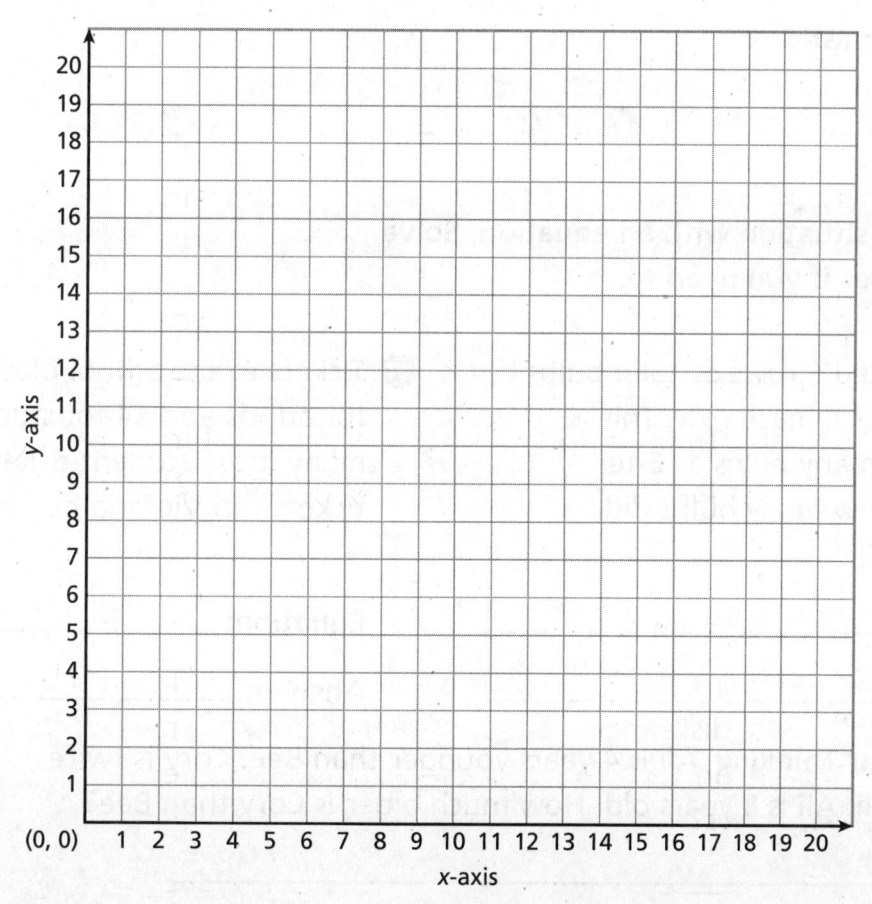

_____

_____

_____

x	y

1-15 Remembering

Complete each Factor Puzzle.

1
32	20
	35

2
	28
36	16

3
2	
18	63

Solve each proportion.

4 $24:28 = n:35$

$n =$ _____

5 $16:b :: 10:35$

$b =$ _____

6 $2:9 = 8:c$

$c =$ _____

Write the basic ratio.

7 $36:81$ _____

8 $25:40$ _____

9 $24:64$ _____

Represent the situation with an equation. Solve. Use parentheses if you need to.

10 Brian planted 6 rows of tulip bulbs with 5 bulbs in each row. This is 3 times as many bulbs as Ester planted. How many bulbs did Ester plant?

Equation: _____

Answer: _____

11 Tickets to the school play cost $6 for adults and $4 for students. How many more student tickets than adult tickets can Victoria buy for $24?

Equation: _____

Answer: _____

12 Stretch Your Thinking Ali is 4 years younger than Bee. Cory is twice as old as Ali. Ali is 8 years old. How much older is Cory than Bee?

Equation: _____

Answer: _____

30 UNIT 1 LESSON 15

2-1 Homework

Name _____ Date _____

Find the perimeter and area of each rectangle or square.

1 3 cm, 5 cm

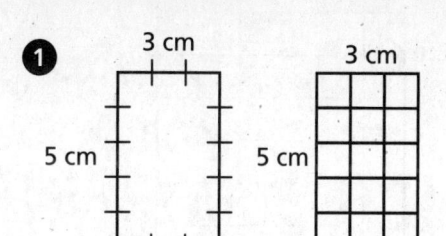

P = _____
A = _____

2 3 cm, 3 cm

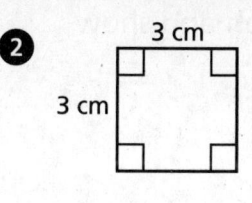

P = _____
A = _____

3 8 cm, 5 cm

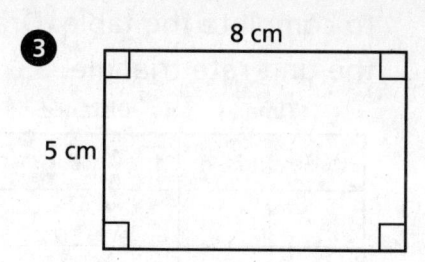

P = _____
A = _____

Find the unknown side length.

4 b, 6 cm, A = 18 cm²

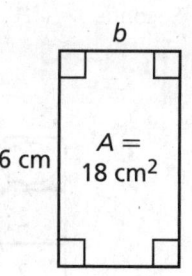

b = _____

5 7 cm, h, A = 14 cm²

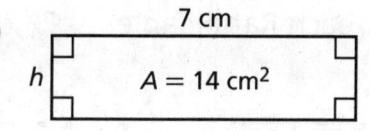

h = _____

6 s, s, A = 49 cm²

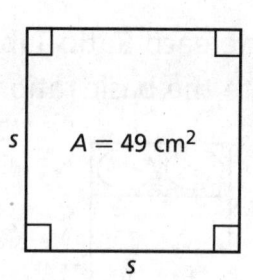

s = _____

Solve.

7 Kaya is wallpapering one wall of her room. The wall is 10 ft long and 8 ft tall. How many square feet of wallpaper will Kaya need? _____

8 Mia's room is 12 ft long and 10 ft wide. She wants to put a border at the top of the walls. How many feet of border does she need? _____

9 A rectangular wall measures 15 ft along the floor. The area of the wall is 180 ft². What is the height of the wall?

_____

10 Corey is tiling a rectangular bathroom that is 6 ft by 8 ft. Each tile covers 2 ft². How many tiles will he need?

_____

UNIT 2 LESSON 1 — Units of Area **31**

2-1 Remembering

1 Circle the unit rate in the table. Use the unit rate to complete the table. Draw the graph and show the unit rate triangle.

Time	Distance
Seconds	Yards
1	2
	10
3	
2	
	8

2 Circle each Ratio Table. For each Ratio Table, write the basic ratio.

A.
3 : 5
6 : 10
9 : 15
15 : 20
18 : 25

B.
2 : 3
4 : 6
6 : 9
8 : 12
10 : 15

C.
4 : 9
8 : 18
12 : 27
16 : 36
20 : 45

D.
2 : 6
2 : 8
3 : 9
4 : 12
5 : 15

Use a Factor Puzzle to solve the problem.

3 To make pink paint, Brianna mixed 8 cans of red paint and 14 cans of white paint. She has 20 more cans of red paint. How many cans of white paint does she need to mix in to get the same color pink?

_____ cans

4 **Stretch Your Thinking** Natalie and Dan both start saving money at the same time and both save at their own constant rates. When Dan has saved $6, Natalie has saved $14. How much more than Dan will Natalie have saved when Dan has saved $15?

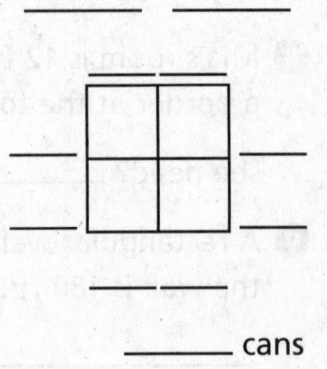

32 UNIT 2 LESSON 1   Units of Area

2-2 Homework

Find the unknown side length.

1. 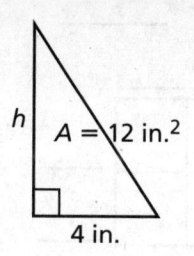 $A = 12$ in.^{2}, base = 4 in.

$h =$ _____

2. 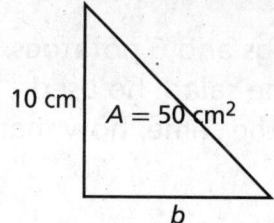 10 cm, $A = 50$ cm^2, base = b

$b =$ _____

3. 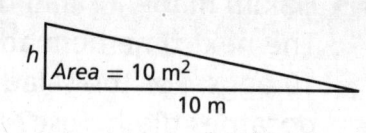 Area = 10 m^2, 10 m

$h =$ _____

Solve.

4. A diagonal divides a square patch of garden that is 2 ft on a side. What is the area on either side of the diagonal?

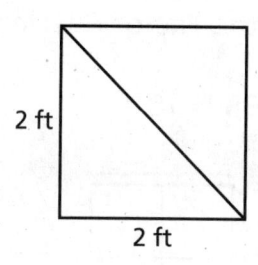

_____

5. A banner in the gym is in the shape of a right triangle. It has a height of 4 ft and a base of 9 ft. What is the area of the banner?

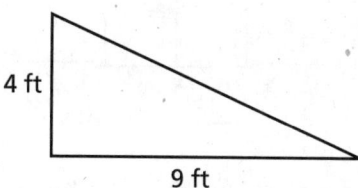

_____

6. A quilt block is made up of 8 right triangles. Each triangle has a 6-inch base and a 6-inch height. How much fabric is needed to cover the back of the quilt block?

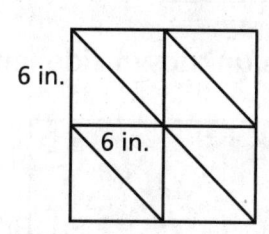

_____

7. Jeremy bought a piece of fabric that has an area of 1,296 in.^{2} He cut it in half diagonally to make two equal triangles. One of the triangles has a height of 24 inches. How long is the base?

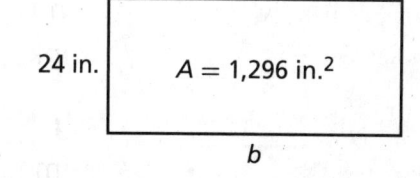

_____

UNIT 2 LESSON 2 — Area of Any Right Triangle 33

2-2 Remembering

Use a Factor Puzzle to solve the problem.

1. Hakim made a salad using 4 eggs and 6 potatoes. The next time he made the same salad, he used 10 eggs. For the salad to taste the same, how many potatoes did he use?

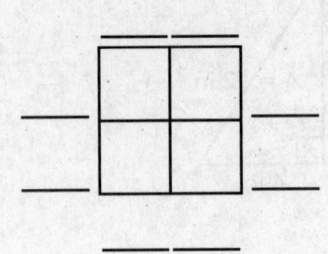

_____ potatoes

Show the Factor Puzzle for each proportion. Solve the proportion.

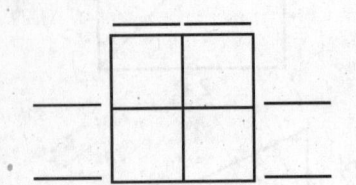

2. $14:35 = 18:a$

    a = _____

3. $b:63 = 8:14$

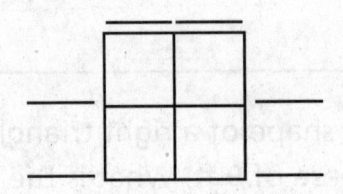

    b = _____

4. $27:45 = 21:c$

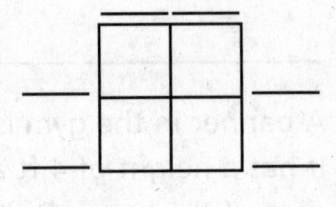

    c = _____

Find the unknown side length.

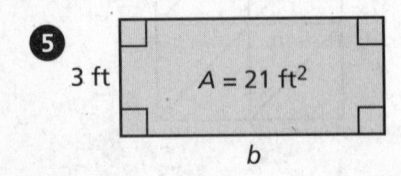

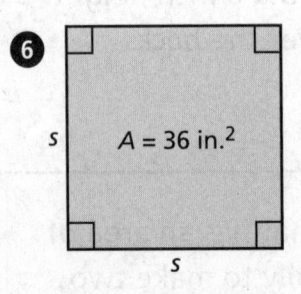

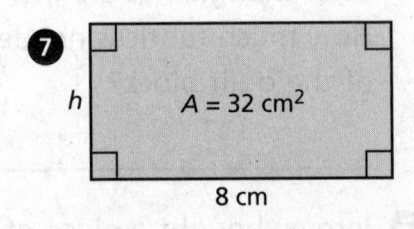

5. 3 ft, $A = 21 \text{ ft}^2$, b

    b = _____

6. s, $A = 36 \text{ in.}^2$, s

    s = _____

7. h, $A = 32 \text{ cm}^2$, 8 cm

    h = _____

8. **Stretch Your Thinking** Find the area of the shaded part of this square. Describe your method.

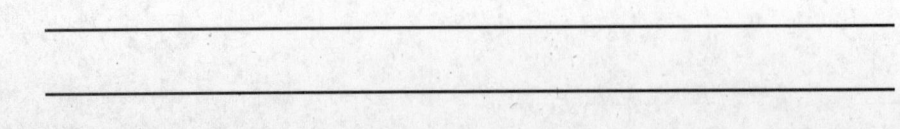

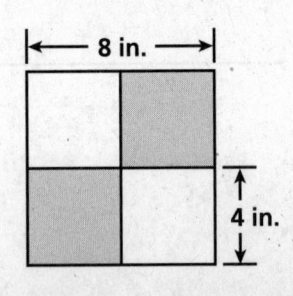

    _____

    _____

    8 in., 4 in.

34 UNIT 2 LESSON 2   Area of Any Right Triangle

2-3 Homework

1 Look at the parallelograms. Which two parallelograms have the same area? Show your work.

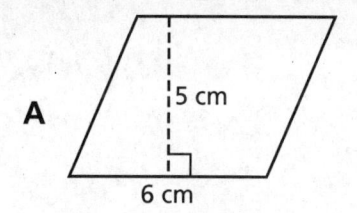

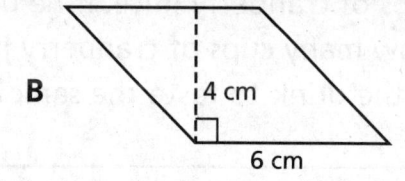

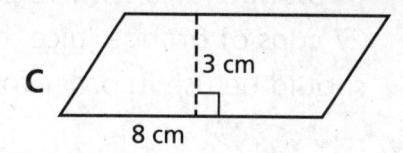

A: height 5 cm, base 6 cm
B: height 4 cm, base 6 cm
C: height 3 cm, base 8 cm

A = _____   A = _____   A = _____

Find the unknown side length.

2 Area = 48 cm², base = 8 cm, height = h

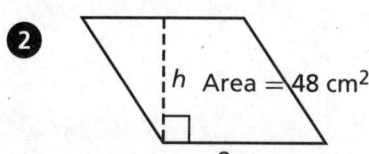

h = _____

3 height = 9 cm, Area = 99 cm², base = b

b = _____

4 Area = 96 cm², height = 8 cm, base = b

b = _____

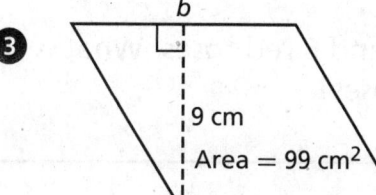

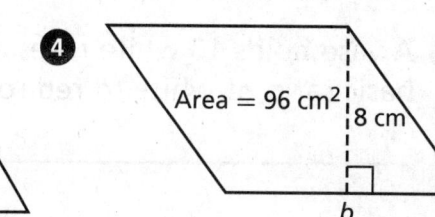

5 Jo designed a flowerbed shaped like a parallelogram. The flowerbed has an area of 475 in.² and a base of 25 in. What is the height of Jo's flowerbed?

_____

Use the landscape design for Exercises 6–8. Show your work.

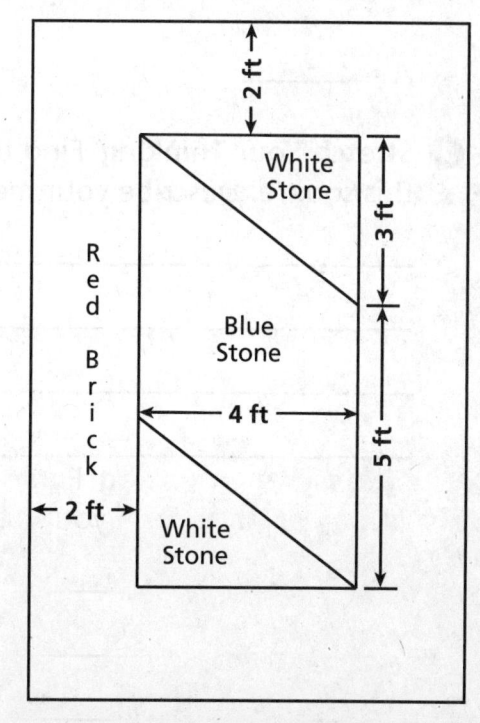

6 How many square feet will the white stone cover in the landscape design?

_____

7 There is a 2-foot border of brick, as shown around the design. How many square feet will the brick cover in the landscape design?

_____

8 What is the perimeter of the landscape design?

_____

Landscape Design:
- 2 ft (top border)
- White Stone (top right)
- 3 ft
- Red Brick (left side)
- Blue Stone (middle)
- 4 ft
- 5 ft
- 2 ft (bottom)
- White Stone (bottom right)

UNIT 2 LESSON 3   Area of Any Parallelogram 35

2-3 Remembering

Solve.

Show your work.

1. Brendan makes a cranberry-orange drink by mixing 15 cups of orange juice with 10 cups of cranberry juice. If he uses 27 cups of orange juice, how many cups of cranberry juice should he use in order for the drink to taste the same?

   _____

2. What is the basic ratio of red to white for a paint mixture of 14 pints of red paint and 35 pints of white paint?

   _____

3. A vase holds 10 white roses and 6 red roses. What is the basic ratio of white to red roses?

   _____

Find the area of each right triangle.

4. 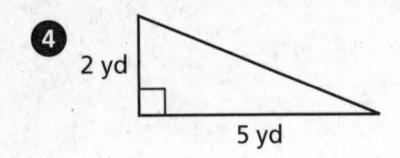 2 yd, 5 yd

   A = _____

5. 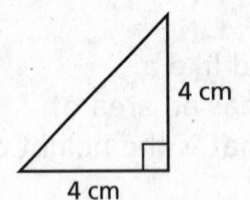 4 cm, 4 cm

   A = _____

6. 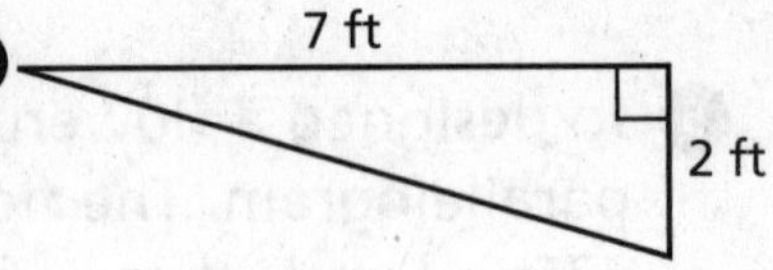 7 ft, 2 ft

   A = _____

7. **Stretch Your Thinking** Find the area of the shaded part of this square. Describe your method.

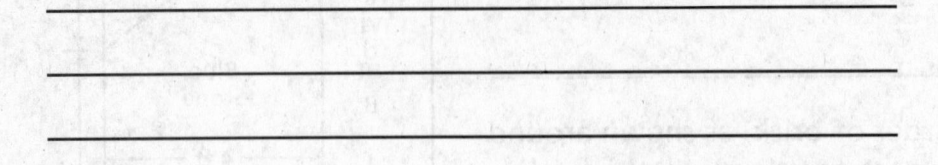

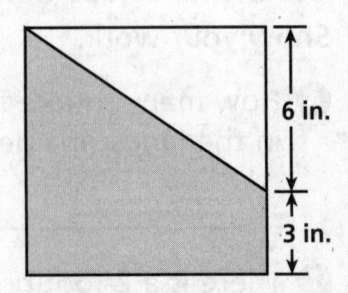

   _____
   _____
   _____
   _____

   6 in., 3 in.

36 UNIT 2 LESSON 3 — Area of Any Parallelogram

2-4 Homework

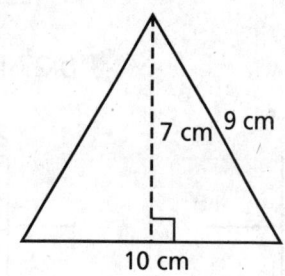

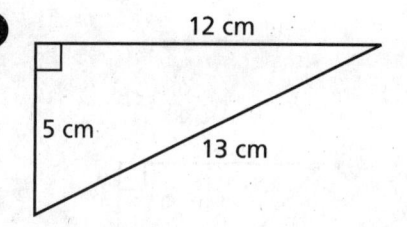

Find the area of each triangle.

1. Triangle with height 9 cm and base 10 cm.

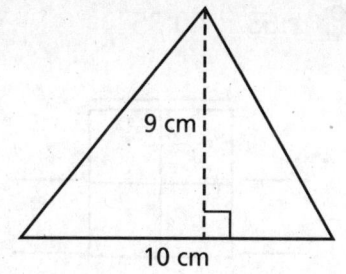

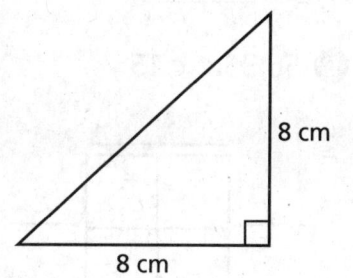

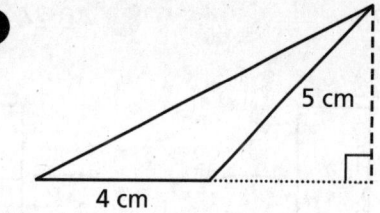

2. Triangle with height 5 cm and base 4 cm.

3. Right triangle with legs 8 cm and 8 cm.

4. Triangle with height 7 cm, side 9 cm, and base 10 cm.

5. Right triangle with legs 5 cm and 12 cm, hypotenuse 13 cm.

6. Triangle with height 6 cm, side 7 cm, and side 8 cm.

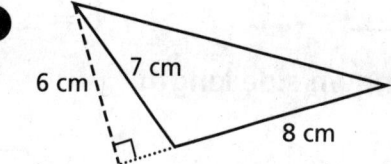

7. An art project requires a triangular piece of cardboard having a base measure of 10 cm and a height of 6 cm. What is the area of a triangular face of the cardboard?

8. Brittany and Will each made a triangular sign with an area of 8 ft². The base of Brittany's triangle is half as long as the base of Will's. How do the heights of the triangles compare?

UNIT 2 LESSON 4   Area of Any Triangle 37

2-4 Remembering

Use a Factor Puzzle to solve each proportion.

1. 30:25 :: 42:x

   x = _____

2. 40:24 :: 35:y

   y = _____

3. z:63 :: 40:35

   z = _____

4. 14:21 :: 10:a

   a = _____

5. b:27 :: 16:72

   b = _____

6. 56:35 :: c:15

   c = _____

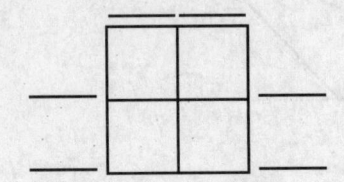

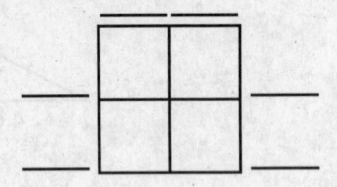

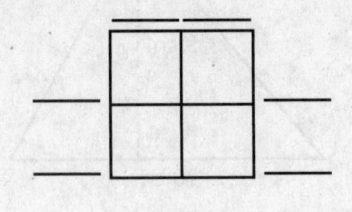

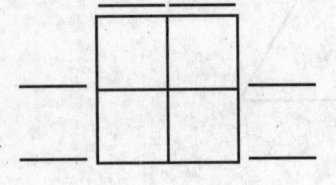

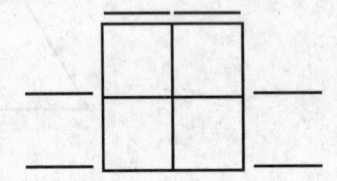

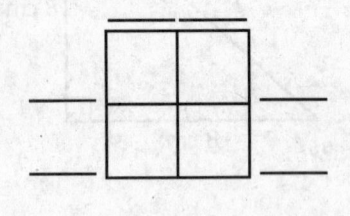

Find the unknown side length.

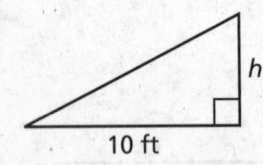

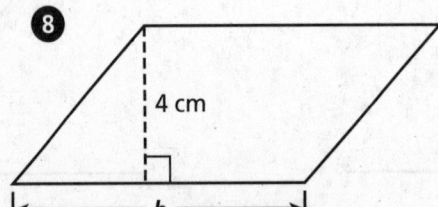

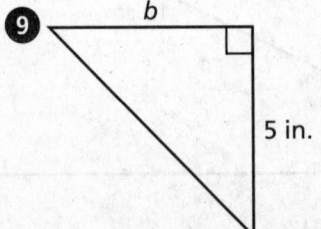

7. (triangle with h and 10 ft)

   $A = 25$ ft²

   h = _____

8. (parallelogram with height 4 cm and base b)

   $A = 36$ cm²

   b = _____

9. (right triangle with b and 5 in.)

   $A = 15$ in.²

   b = _____

10. **Stretch Your Thinking** Find the area of the shaded part of this parallelogram. Describe your method.

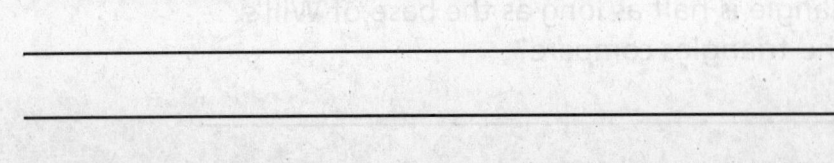

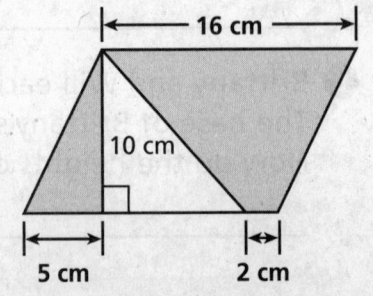

    (parallelogram with top 16 cm, height 10 cm, bottom segments 5 cm and 2 cm)

    _____

    _____

38 UNIT 2 LESSON 4   Area of Any Triangle

2-5 Homework   Name _____   Date _____

Find the perimeter and area.

1 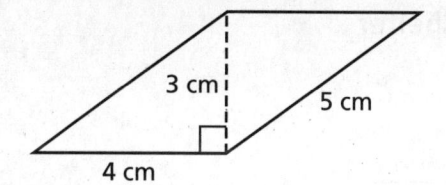 (parallelogram: 3 cm height, 5 cm side, 4 cm base)

P = _____   A = _____

2 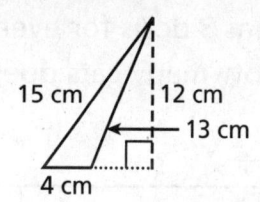 (triangle: 15 cm, 12 cm, 13 cm, 4 cm base)

P = _____   A = _____

3 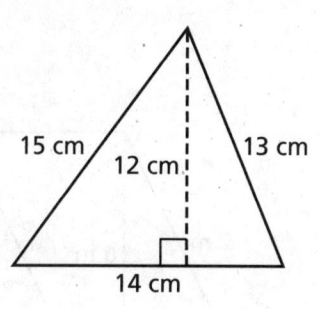 (triangle: 15 cm, 12 cm height, 13 cm, 14 cm base)

P = _____   A = _____

4 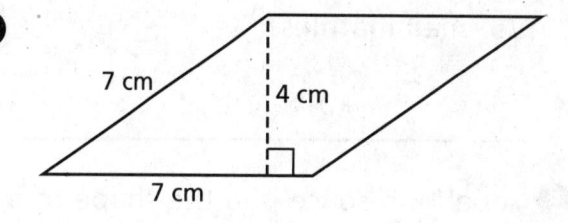 (parallelogram: 7 cm side, 4 cm height, 7 cm base)

P = _____   A = _____

Choose a base and a corresponding height with lengths you can find without a ruler. Then find the area. Each square represents 1 cm².

5 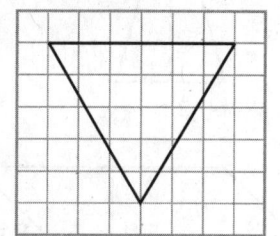 (triangle on grid)

A = _____

6 (parallelogram on grid)

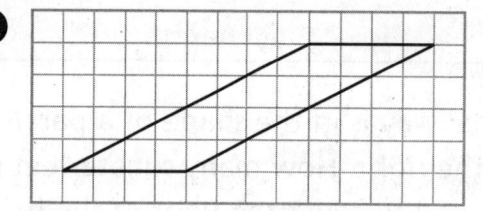

A = _____

7 A baseball diamond has an area of 3,600 ft². What is the distance between each base? How far does a runner run around the bases when hitting a home run?

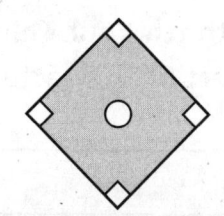

_____

8 A postcard in the shape of a parallelogram has an area of 12 in.². What are two possible lengths of bases and heights for the postcard?

_____

UNIT 2 LESSON 5   Select the Needed Measurements **39**

2-5 Remembering

Solve.

1. A pet shelter has 3 dogs for every 2 cats. If the shelter has 15 dogs, how many cats does it have?

   _____

2. Ten large marbles weigh the same as 14 small marbles. How many large marbles weigh the same as 35 small marbles?

   _____

3. A parking space is in the shape of a parallelogram as shown at the right. What is the area of the parking space?

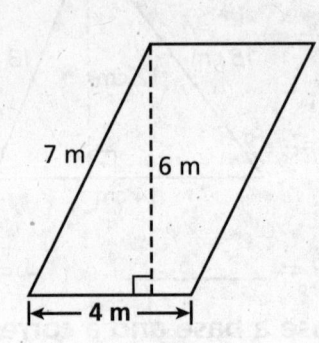

   _____

4. Kevin has a triangular kite that is 3 feet wide and has an area of 6 square feet. How tall is the kite?

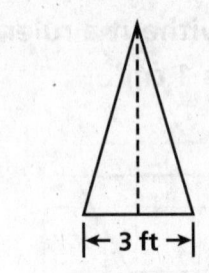

   _____

5. A hallway is in the shape of a parallelogram as shown at the right. How many square feet of carpet are needed to cover the floor of the hallway?

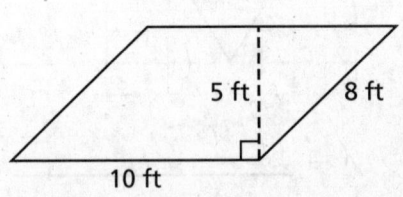

   _____

6. **Stretch Your Thinking** Find the area of the shaded part of this rectangle. Describe your method.

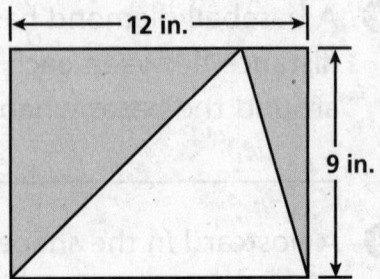

   _____
   _____
   _____

40 UNIT 2 LESSON 5 — Select the Needed Measurements

2-6 Homework Name _____ Date _____

Find the area.

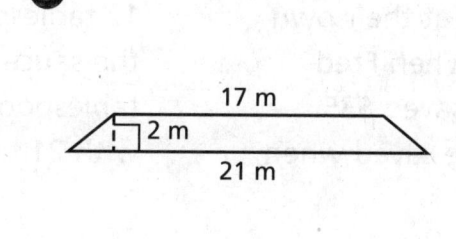

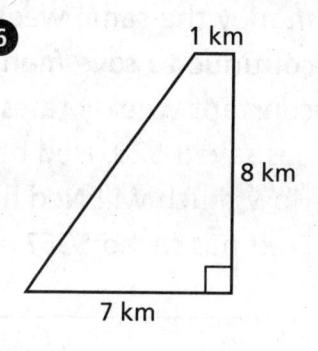

1. (trapezoid: top 7 yd, left side 6 yd, bottom 9 yd)

2. (trapezoid: top 11 ft, height 4 ft, bottom 15 ft)

3. (trapezoid: top 2 in., height 6 in., bottom 10 in.)

4. (trapezoid: top 19 cm, height 20 cm, bottom 15 cm)

5. (trapezoid: height 2 m, bottom 21 m, top 17 m)

6. (trapezoid: top 1 km, right side 8 km, bottom 7 km)

7. A playground is in the shape of an isosceles trapezoid. The top base is 10 ft. The bottom base is 42 ft. The height is 12 ft. A slanted side is 20 ft. What is the distance around the playground?

8. One part of the roof of a house is in the form of an isosceles trapezoid. The bottom base is 28 feet long. The top base is 6 feet long, and the height is 16 feet. What is the area of this portion of the roof?

9. A place mat is in the form of an isosceles trapezoid. One base of the trapezoid is 17 inches long, and the other base is 13 inches long. The height is 12 inches. What is the area of the place mat?

UNIT 2 LESSON 6   Area of Any Trapezoid **41**

2-6 Remembering

Solve.

1. In the library, there are 4 printers and 10 computers. If the ratio stays the same, how many printers will there be when there are 35 computers?

   _____

2. An art club has 12 girls and 15 boys. A chess club has the same ratio of girls to boys as the art club. If there are 8 girls in the chess club, how many boys are there?

   _____

3. Ned and Fred both start saving money the same week and both continue to save money at their own constant weekly rates. When Fred has saved $28, Ned has saved $35. How much will Ned have saved when Fred has saved $36?

   _____

4. Sarah makes a sauce by mixing 8 tablespoons of honey with 12 tablespoons of mustard. To make the sauce taste the same, how many tablespoons of honey should she mix with 21 tablespoons of mustard?

   _____

Find the unknown side length.

5. (parallelogram: 7 m, 6 m, 7 m, b)

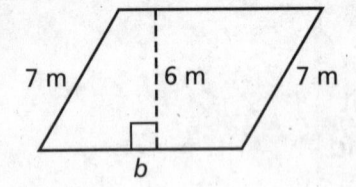

   $A = 54$ m²

   $b =$ _____

6. (triangle: 10 in., 10 in., h, 12 in.)

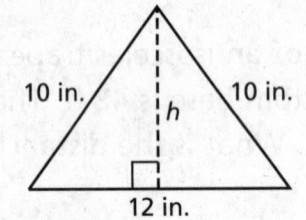

   $A = 48$ in.²

   $h =$ _____

7. (right triangle: h, 10 mi, 6 mi)

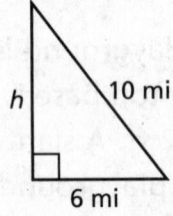

   $P = 24$ mi

   $h =$ _____

8. **Stretch Your Thinking** Find the area of the white rhombus. Describe your method.

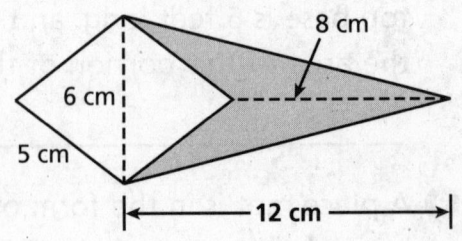

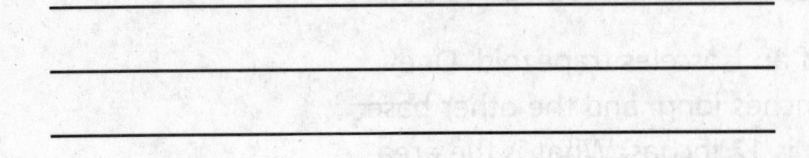

   (figure: 8 cm, 6 cm, 5 cm, 12 cm)

   _____

   _____

   _____

   _____

42 UNIT 2 LESSON 6 — Area of Any Trapezoid

2-7 Homework

Find the perimeter and area.

1. [figure: 2 yd top, 3 yd diagonal, 2 yd, 3 yd left, 2 yd right, 6 yd bottom]

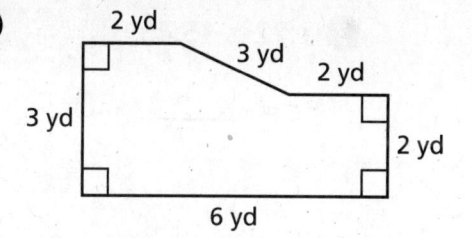

   P = _____   A = _____

2. [figure: 5 cm, 4 cm, 2 cm, 9 cm]

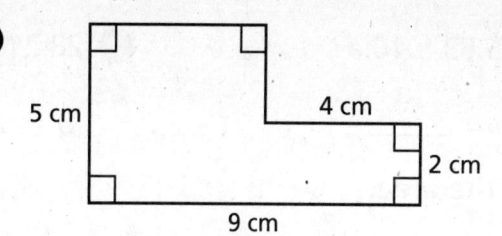

   P = _____   A = _____

3. [figure: 6 cm, 1 cm, 2 cm, 2 cm, 3 cm, 3 cm]

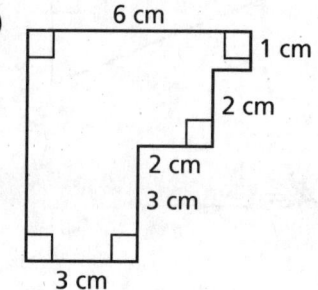

   P = _____   A = _____

4. [figure: 4 cm, 3 cm, 5 cm, 3 cm, 5 cm, 4 cm]

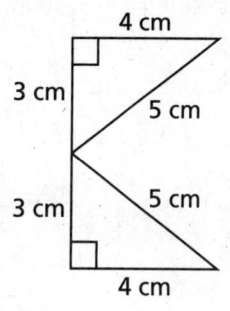

   P = _____   A = _____

Find the area of the shaded part.

5. [figure: rectangle CDEF, CD = 6 ft, CF = 3 ft] CDEF is a rectangle with an area of 24 ft².

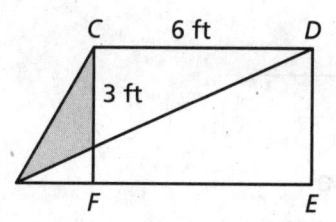

   A = _____

6. [figure: triangle, 8 cm, 4 cm, 10 cm, 6 cm]

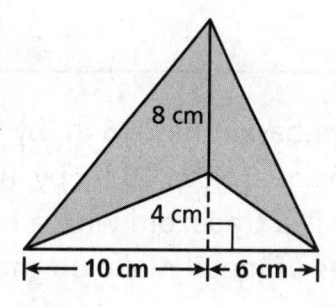

   A = _____

Solve.

7. Paul is making a birdhouse with the measurements shown on the drawing at the right. What is the area of the back of the birdhouse?

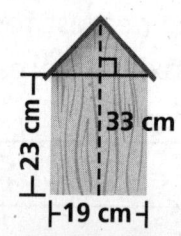

   [figure: 23 cm, 33 cm, 19 cm]

   _____

8. How much metal will be needed to make 4 of the signs shown at the right?

   [figure: 30 in., 15 in., 30 in.]

UNIT 2 LESSON 7   Area of a Complex Figure **43**

2-7 Remembering

Solve each proportion.

① 45:63 :: 10:a

a = _____

② 28:21 :: 20:b

b = _____

③ c:72 :: 15:45

c = _____

Find the area.

④ 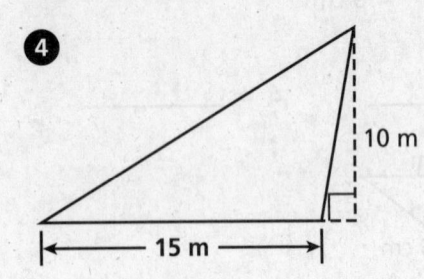 (triangle with height 10 m and base 15 m)

A = _____

⑤ 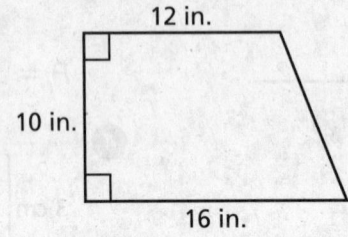 (trapezoid with top 12 in., height 10 in., bottom 16 in.)

A = _____

⑥ (triangle with base 5 cm and height 4 cm)

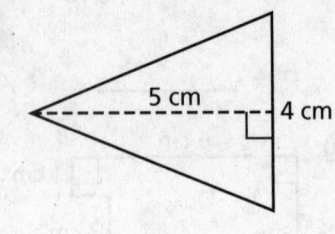

A = _____

Solve.

⑦ A quilt piece is in the shape of a trapezoid. The top parallel side measures 4 cm and the bottom parallel side measures 8 cm. The height is 5 cm. What is the area of the quilt piece?

_____

⑧ A metal wastebasket has a 6 in. by 6 in. square bottom and an open square top 10 in. by 10 in. Each side of the wastebasket is a trapezoid with a height of 12 in. How many square inches of metal make up the wastebasket?

_____

⑨ **Stretch Your Thinking** The measurements given are rounded to the nearest foot. Use these measurements to find the approximate area of the trapezoid. Describe your method.

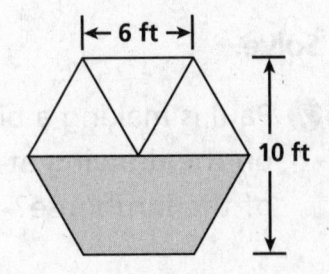

(figure: hexagon-like shape, 6 ft wide at top, 10 ft tall)

_____
_____
_____
_____

44 UNIT 2 LESSON 7 — Area of a Complex Figure

2-8 Homework

Find the perimeter and area.

1. Octagon, apothem 10 ft, side 8 ft.

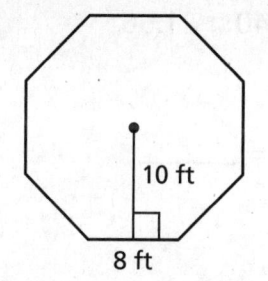

P = _____

A = _____

2. Pentagon, apothem 3 in., side 4 in.

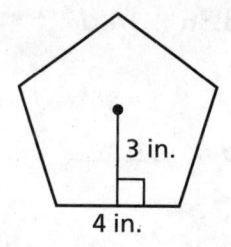

P = _____

A = _____

3. Hexagon, apothem 4 yd, side 5 yd.

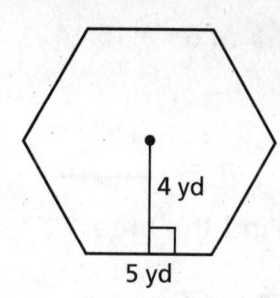

P = _____

A = _____

4. Pentagon, apothem 6 m, side 9 m.

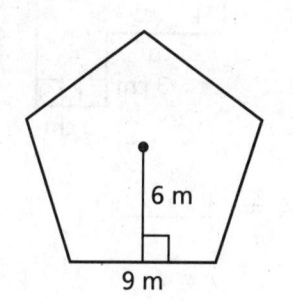

P = _____

A = _____

5. Hexagon, apothem 6 cm, side 7 cm.

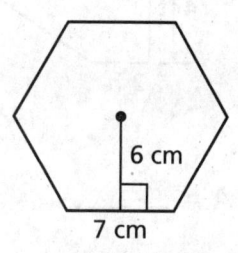

P = _____

A = _____

6. Octagon, apothem 7 km, side 6 km.

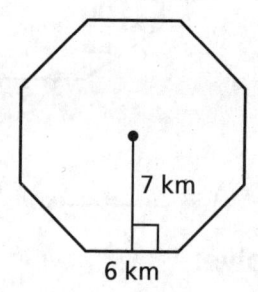

P = _____

A = _____

Solve.

7. Talia made a pattern for a potholder that is a regular 12–sided polygon. The perimeter of the potholder pattern is 36 in. The distance to the center is 6 in. to the nearest in. What is the area of the potholder to the nearest in.^{2}?

_____

8. A house number is displayed on a plaque in the shape of a regular 7-sided polygon. The area of the plaque is 70 in.^{2} The perpendicular distance from a side to the center is 5 in. to the nearest inch. What is the perimeter of the plaque?

_____

UNIT 2 LESSON 8 — Area of Any Regular Polygon

2-8 Remembering

Solve each proportion.

① $m:63 :: 16:14$

$m = \_\_\_\_$

② $8:36 :: 14:d$

$d = \_\_\_\_$

③ $n:40 :: 21:56$

$n = \_\_\_\_$

Find the area.

④

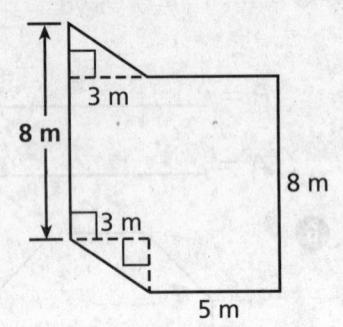

$A = \_\_\_\_$

⑤

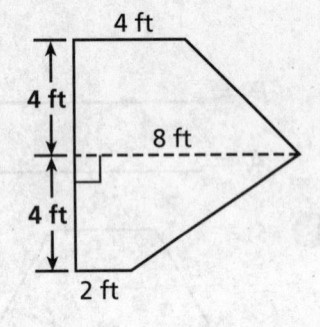

$A = \_\_\_\_$

⑥

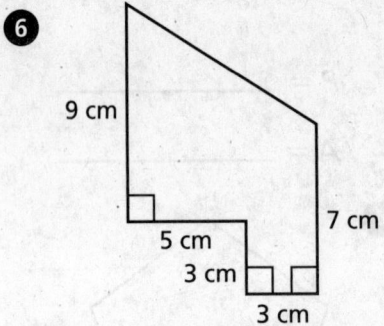

$A = \_\_\_\_$

Solve.

⑦ Alexandra wants to carpet her bedroom. The floor plan of the bedroom is shown at the right. How many square feet of carpet are needed to cover the floor of the bedroom including the closet?

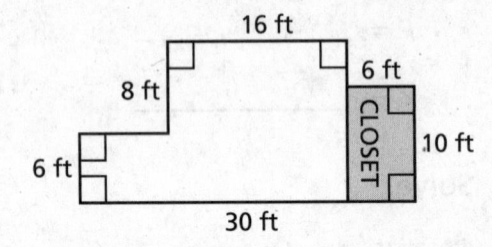

⑧ **Stretch Your Thinking** Find the area of the shaded part of the figure. Describe your method.

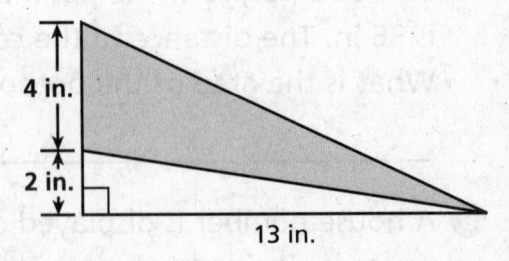

46 UNIT 2 LESSON 8   Area of Any Regular Polygon

2-9 Homework

1. Plot these points on the coordinate plane at the right: A(1,6), B(1,10). Plot point C to make a right triangle with base BC measuring 3 units long. What ordered pair locates point C?

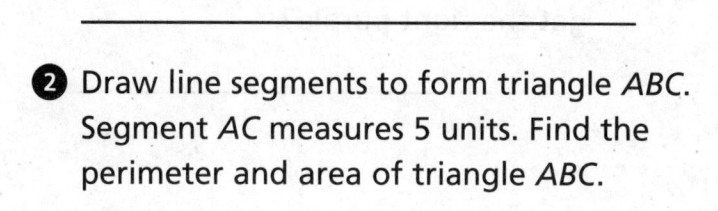

   _____

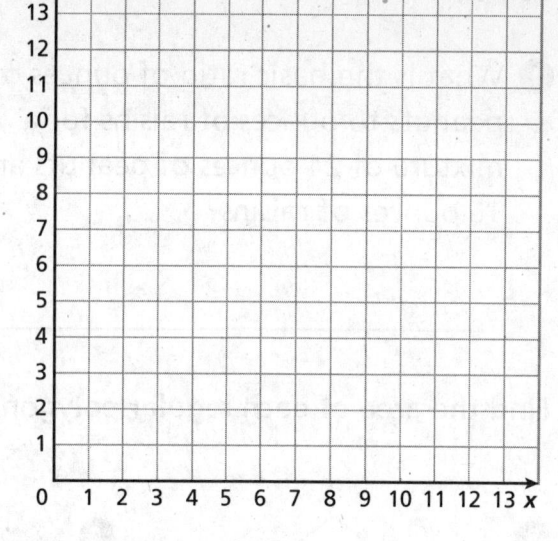

2. Draw line segments to form triangle ABC. Segment AC measures 5 units. Find the perimeter and area of triangle ABC.

   P = _____   A = _____

3. Plot these ordered pairs: D(2,2), E(5,6), F(11,6). Plot point G, so polygon DEFG is a parallelogram. What ordered pair locates point G?

   _____

4. Draw line segments to form parallelogram DEFG. Segment DE is 5 units long. Find the perimeter and area of parallelogram DEFG.

   P = _____   A = _____

5. A tile installer is planning how many blue and white tiles are needed to tile a floor. Each tile is 6 in. high and 4 in. wide. Every other tile will be blue. Each unit on the grid represents 1 in. The bottom left corner of the first blue tile is at (0, 0). How many blue tiles will there be in a section 24 in. long and 24 in. wide? Explain.

   _____
   _____
   _____

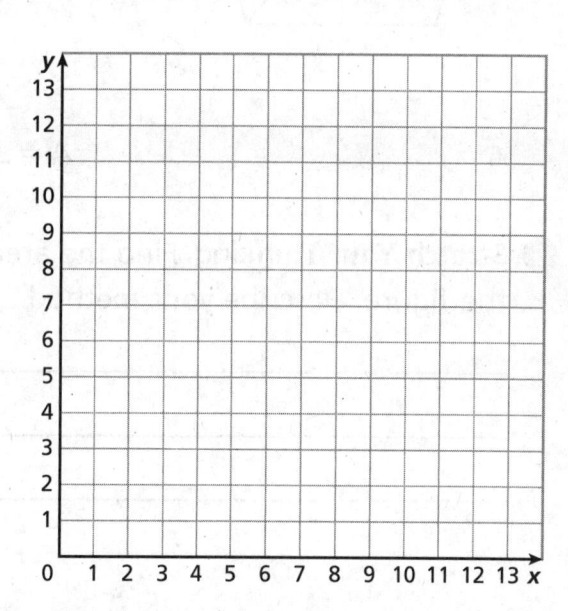

6. An archaeologist roped off a rectangular excavation site that is located on a coordinate grid. The vertices of the site are (2,5), (2,11), (12,11), and (12,5). If the units are in meters, what is the area of the site?

   A = _____

UNIT 2 LESSON 9   Graph Polygons in the Coordinate Plane **47**

2-9 Remembering

Solve.

1. What is the basic ratio of ounces of peanuts to ounces of raisins for a mixture of 24 ounces of peanuts and 16 ounces of raisins?

_____

2. The basic ratio of blue to red for Ben's favorite purple paint is 4:7. How many quarts of blue paint should be mixed with 21 quarts of red paint to get the right purple?

_____

Find the area of each regular polygon.

3. 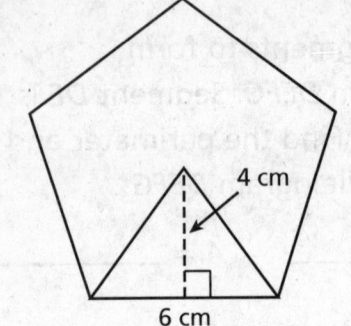 (regular pentagon, apothem 4 cm, side 6 cm)

A = _____

4. 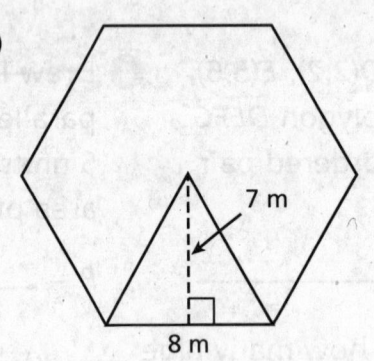 (regular hexagon, apothem 7 m, side 8 m)

A = _____

5. 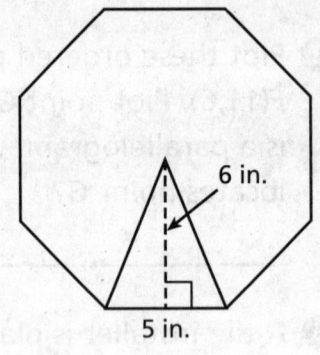 (regular octagon, apothem 6 in., side 5 in.)

A = _____

6. Stretch Your Thinking Find the area of the shaded part of the figure. Describe your method.

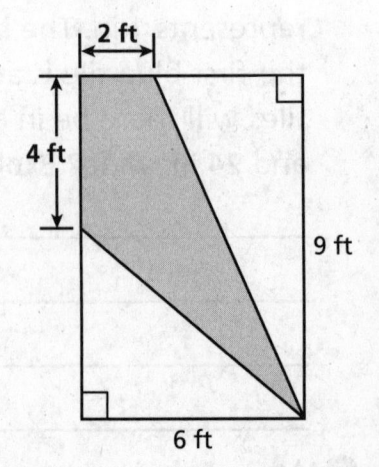

_____
_____
_____

2-10 Homework

Name _____ **Date** _____

All figures in the tessellation below are regular figures. Use a pattern to color this tessellation.

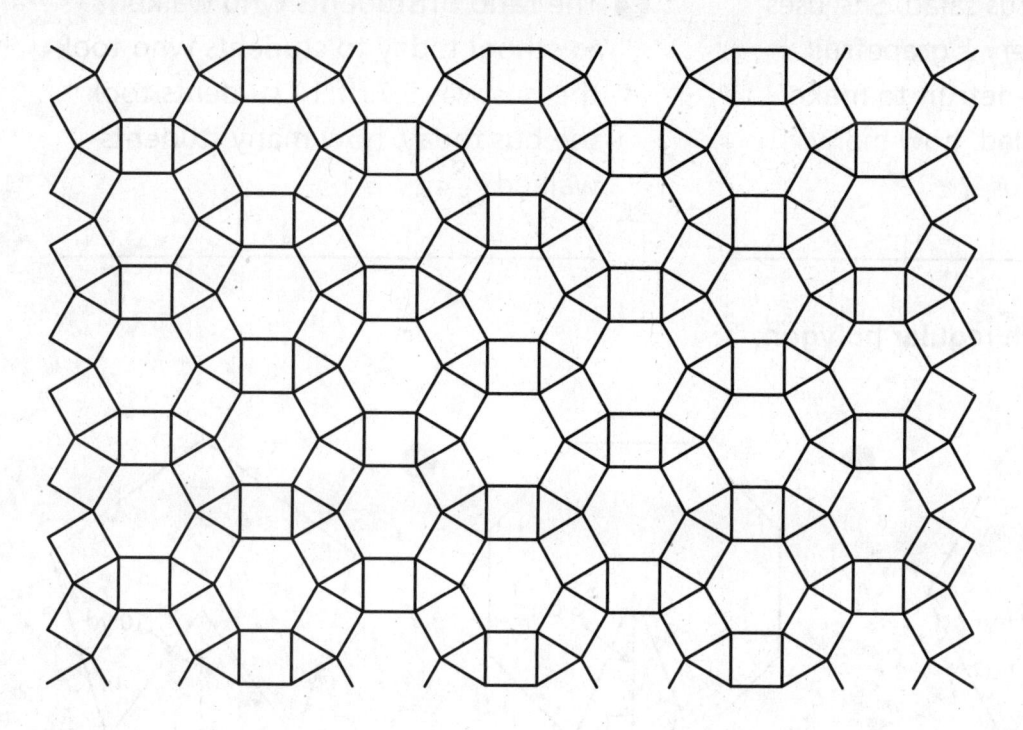

1 Describe the pattern you used to color the tessellation.

_____

_____

2 Does your colored tessellation have a line of symmetry? That is, can you find a line to fold it on so all the shapes match exactly? Do the colors match when you fold it on that line?

_____

_____

3 Choose a color in your tessellation. Estimate the area covered by that color in cm^2.

_____

UNIT 2 LESSON 10 ・ Focus on Mathematical Practices

2-10 Remembering

Name _____ Date _____

Solve.

① Jane makes a citrus salad. She uses 3 oranges for every 2 grapefruit. If she uses 12 grapefruit to make an extra large salad, how many oranges will she use?

_____

② The ratio of students who walked to school today to students who took the bus was 5:7. If 14 students took the bus today, how many students walked?

_____

Find the area of each regular polygon.

③ 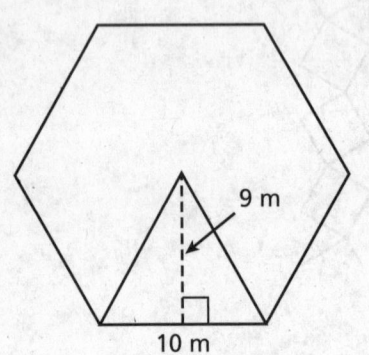 (hexagon with apothem 9 m, side 10 m)

A = _____

④ 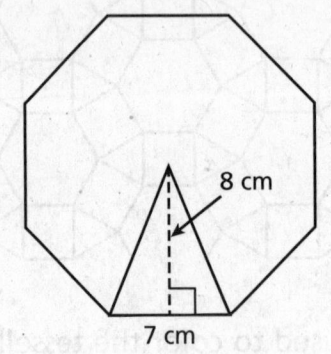 (octagon with apothem 8 cm, side 7 cm)

A = _____

⑤ (pentagon with apothem 10 yd, side 15 yd)

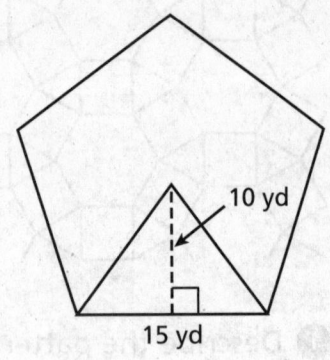

A = _____

⑥ **Stretch Your Thinking** Find the area of the shaded part of the figure. Describe your method.

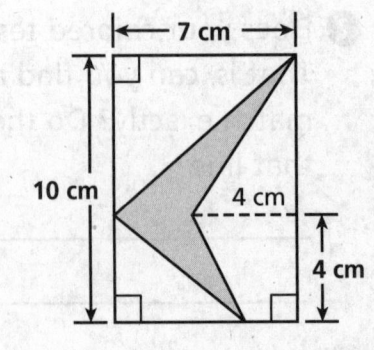

_____
_____
_____
_____

(rectangle 7 cm by 10 cm with shaded triangle, 4 cm and 4 cm marked)

3-1 Homework

Divide. Give your answer as a quotient with a remainder.

1. 9)372
2. 32)2,190
3. 8)582
4. 59)2,361

5. 23)1,577
6. 47)4,003
7. 84)9,415
8. 19)1,062

Solve. *Show your work.*

9. A company spent $2,415 on plane tickets for 7 employees. All the tickets cost the same amount. How much did each ticket cost?

10. A theater seats 496 people. If all 8 performances to a play sell out, how many people will see the play?

11. The marching band raised $2,499 from a raffle and cookie sale. Each of the 48 band members will get an equal share of the money to put toward a new uniform. How much money will each band member get? How many cents will be left over?

UNIT 3 LESSON 1 — Place Value and Whole Number Division 51

3-1 Remembering

Name _____ Date _____

1. Damond is buying packages of construction paper. In each package there are 6 white sheets and 18 colored sheets. How many colored sheets does he buy if he buys 14 white sheets?

   _____

2. Julia is making a necklace that has 8 red beads for every 12 blue beads. How many red beads will she use if she uses 27 blue beads?

   _____

Find the perimeter and area of each figure.

3. Rectangle: 16 cm by 9 cm

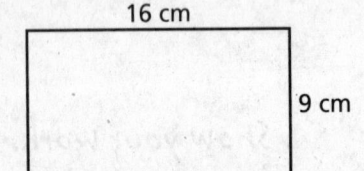

   P = _____
   A = _____

4. Right triangle with legs 8 ft and 6 ft, hypotenuse 10 ft

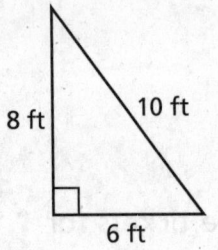

   P = _____
   A = _____

5. Pentagon with base 12 yd and height 8 yd

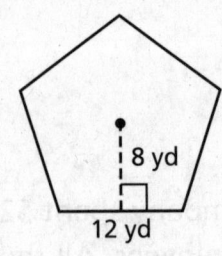

   P = _____
   A = _____

6. Marylin is cutting a triangular banner out of felt. The banner is 4 feet high and has a base of 3 feet. How much felt does Marylin need for the banner?

   _____

7. **Stretch Your Thinking** Natalia and her friends raised money for charity. The amount they raised is shown in the table. They pooled their money and divided it equally among four charities. How much money did they give to each charity?

   _____

Friend	Amount Raised
Natalia	$18
Juan	$21
Stephen	$37
Jawan	$43

Place Value and Whole Number Division

3-2 Homework

Solve. *Show your work.*

1. Joshua cashed a check for $16.79. He asked the teller to give him as many quarters as possible. How many quarters did he get?

   _____

2. The tallest tree in the world is a redwood in Redwood National and State Parks. It is 379 feet tall. How many yards is this?

   _____

3. Emergency workers in a small city estimate that, in the event of a hurricane, they will need to transport 3,250 people out of the city on buses. If each bus holds 48 people, how many buses will they need?

   _____

4. On Tuesday, a company bottled 4,775 bottles of water and packaged them into as many 6-packs as possible. How many bottles were left over?

   _____

5. A landscaping company bought 732 kilograms of mulch. If they bought 40 bags of mulch in all, what is the mass of each bag?

   _____

Divide. Give your answers to the nearest cent.

6. 36)$117   7. 85)$380   8. 62)$729   9. 18)$402

3-2 Remembering

1. Michelle is mixing paint. She mixes 5 cups red for every 3 cups blue to make purple. How many cups of red should she use if she uses 15 cups of blue?

   _____

2. For every 15 minutes Jason spends practicing the piano, he spends 10 minutes practicing the trumpet. If Jason spends 30 minutes practicing the piano, how many minutes does he spend practicing the trumpet?

   _____

Find the perimeter and area of each figure.

3. Triangle with sides 13 mi, 13 mi, base 10 mi, height 12 mi.

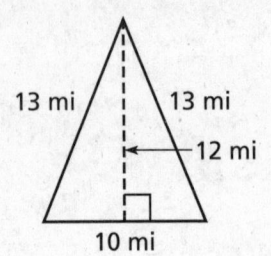

   P = _____

   A = _____

4. Trapezoid with top 16 m, left side 8 m, right side 10 m, bottom 4 m, height 5 m.

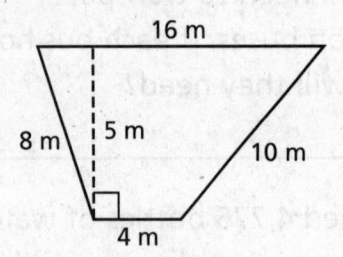

   P = _____

   A = _____

5. Octagon with apothem 10 in. and side 8 in.

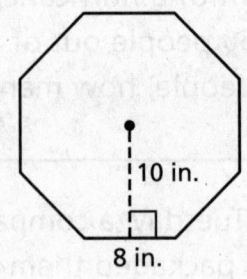

   P = _____

   A = _____

6. Barry needs 56 square feet of mulch to cover his garden. The width of the garden is 8 feet. What is the length of the garden?

   _____

7. **Stretch Your Thinking** There are 113 girls and 121 boys in the marching band. The routine the band is practicing has all of the musicians standing in equal rows. If the number of rows is between 10 and 15, how many rows are there? How many musicians are standing in each row?

   _____

3-3 Homework

Name _____ Date _____

Multiply

① 413 · 0.02   ② 0.6 · 801   ③ 32.5 · 0.5   ④ 4 · 6.63

_____   _____   _____   _____

⑤ 0.12
× 12

⑥ 5.9
× 4.4

⑦ 6.1
× 0.19

⑧ 36
× 0.07

Use the fact that 28 · 63 = 1,764 to find each product.

⑨ 0.28 · 6,300   ⑩ 0.28 · 630   ⑪ 0.28 · 63   ⑫ 28 · 6.3

_____   _____   _____   _____

⑬ 2.8 · 630   ⑭ 2.8 · 63   ⑮ 2.8 · 6.3   ⑯ 28 · 0.63

_____   _____   _____   _____

Multiply

⑰ 0.8 · 0.9   ⑱ 8 · 0.7   ⑲ 0.5 · 6   ⑳ 0.12 · 3

_____   _____   _____   _____

Solve. *Show your work.*

㉑ The Neelys have 87.6 acres of land. The Francos have 0.7 times as much land. How much land do the Francos have?

_____

㉒ Dante bought six CDs for $13.88 each. How much did he spend?

_____

UNIT 3 LESSON 3   Multiplying by a Decimal **55**

3-3 Remembering

1 For every 6 miles Juda runs, Hannah runs 11 miles. If the ratio stays the same, how many miles will Juda run if Hannah runs 44 miles?

_____

2 There is a woodchip area shaped like a trapezoid at the playground at Millie's school. The bases of the trapezoid are 12 feet and 18 feet. The height of the trapezoid is 20 feet. How much of the playground is covered with woodchips?

_____

Divide. Write your answer as a quotient with a remainder.

3 9)877   **4** 78)8,322   **5** 6)403   **6** 16)1,277

7 Ned is using strips of cloth to make scarves. He needs 28 strips for each scarf. If he has 781 strips of cloth, how many scarves can Ned make? How many strips will be left over?

_____

8 Stretch Your Thinking Nancy and Bruce are typing reports. Nancy's report is 12 pages long, and she has typed 0.7 of it. Bruce's report is 9 pages long, and he has typed 0.8 of it. Who has typed more pages?

_____

56 UNIT 3 LESSON 3   Multiplying by a Decimal

3-4 Homework

Divide. Round your answer to the nearest tenth.

1) $0.4 \overline{)6}$
2) $0.08 \overline{)4.2}$
3) $2.4 \overline{)40}$
4) $0.5 \overline{)0.94}$

5) $0.12 \overline{)5.4}$
6) $0.55 \overline{)13}$
7) $7.5 \overline{)6.5}$
8) $0.24 \overline{)8}$

Use the fact that 1,764 ÷ 28 = 63 to find each quotient.

9) $0.28 \overline{)1.764}$
10) $0.28 \overline{)176.4}$
11) $0.28 \overline{)17.64}$
12) $28 \overline{)176.4}$

13) $2.8 \overline{)1,764}$
14) $2.8 \overline{)176.4}$
15) $2.8 \overline{)17.64}$
16) $28 \overline{)17.64}$

Divide. Be careful to consider which number is the divisor.

17) $1.8 \div 0.09$
18) $21 \div 0.7$
19) $3.2 \div 0.8$
20) $0.12 \div 0.04$

Solve.   Show your work.

21) Ronit is buying storage boxes for her CDs. She has 456 CDs. Each box holds 36 CDs. How many boxes will she need?

22) Raul's mom sends him to the farmer's market with $12. She tells him to buy as many avocados as he can and to bring back the change. If avocados are 85¢ each, how much change will he bring back?

UNIT 3 LESSON 4   Decimal Divisors **57**

3-4 Remembering

1 John and Karen are each saving money at their own constant rate. When John has saved $15, Karen has saved $18. How much will Karen have saved when John has saved $45?
_____

Find the area.

2 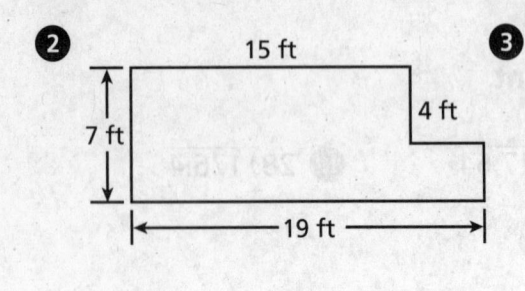
Rectangle with dimensions: 15 ft top, 7 ft left side, 4 ft step down, 19 ft bottom.
A = _____

3 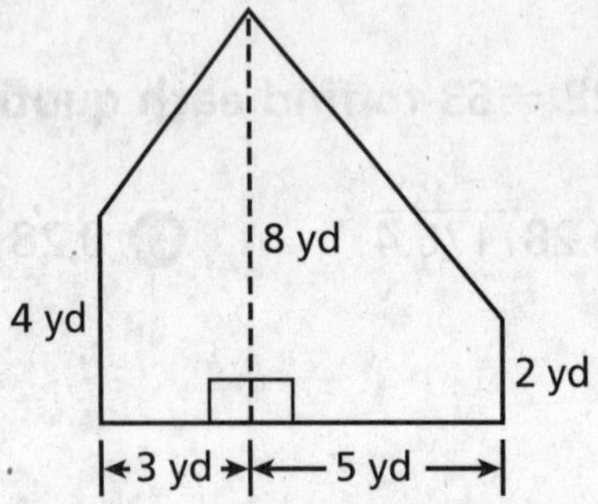
Pentagon/house shape: 8 yd height to peak (dashed), 4 yd, 2 yd right side, base 3 yd + 5 yd.
A = _____

4 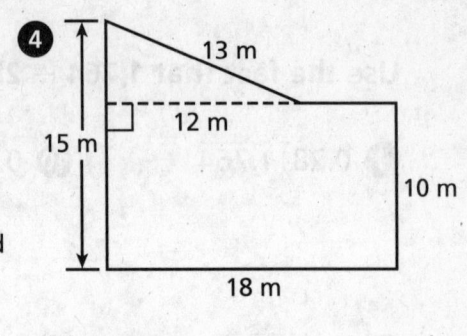
Shape with 13 m top, 12 m (dashed), 15 m left, 10 m right, 18 m bottom.
A = _____

5 Marissa is driving across the country. She drives 1,542 miles in 3 days. She drives the same number of miles each day. How many miles does Marissa drive each day?
_____

6 Joanna can put 24 books in one container. She has to pack 266 books. How many containers does she need to pack all the books?
_____

Use the fact that 45 × 39 = 1,755 to find each product.

7 0.45 · 39

8 4.5 · 0.39

9 4.5 · 3.9

10 0.45 · 0.39

_____ _____ _____ _____

11 Stretch Your Thinking Bottles of water are on sale at two stores. Food Mart is selling 12 bottles for $3.66. Shop Center is selling 6 bottles for $2.10. At which store does it cost less to buy one bottle of water?
_____

58 UNIT 3 LESSON 4 — Decimal Divisors

3-5 Homework

Name _____ Date _____

① Make up a letter Puzzled Penguin might write describing an error made while multiplying or dividing.

Dear Math Students,

_____
_____
_____
_____
_____
_____
_____
_____

Your friend,
Puzzled Penguin

② Write a response to your Puzzled Penguin letter.

_____
_____
_____
_____
_____
_____
_____

UNIT 3 LESSON 5　　　　　　　　　Multiplication or Division　**59**

3-5 Remembering

1 The pet store is selling 9 cans of cat food for $12. At this price, how many cans of cat food can you buy for $32?

_____

Find the unknown side length.

2 Square with h on side, A = 168 cm², base = 14 cm

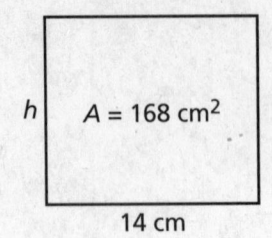

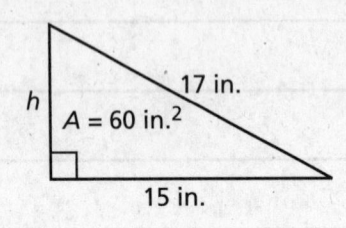

h = _____

3 Right triangle with hypotenuse 17 in., height h, base 15 in., A = 60 in.²

h = _____

4 Parallelogram with A = 1,178 mm², height 19 mm, slant side 25 mm, base b

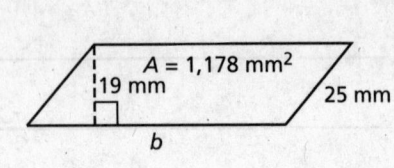

b = _____

Multiply or divide. Round the quotient to the nearest tenth if necessary.

5 5.9 × 2.4

6 0.9)53.1

7 0.56 × 9.7

8 0.28)233.6

9 0.5)2.05

10 125 × 0.6

11 1.9)6.84

12 4.1 × 0.38

13 Stretch Your Thinking Jenny and George combined their allowances to buy the same present for each of their four teachers. Jenny had $13.75. George had $2.26 less than Jenny. How much did one present cost?

_____

60 UNIT 3 LESSON 5

3-6 Homework

Complete each statement with < or >.

1. $\frac{1}{3}$ ◯ $\frac{1}{2}$
2. $\frac{1}{6}$ ◯ $\frac{1}{8}$
3. $\frac{3}{8}$ ◯ $\frac{3}{5}$
4. 0.04 ◯ 0.004

5. $\frac{2}{5}$ ◯ $\frac{2}{3}$
6. $\frac{7}{10}$ ◯ $\frac{7}{8}$
7. 0.2 ◯ 0.02
8. 0.03 ◯ 0.3

9. $5\frac{3}{8}$ ◯ $6\frac{5}{8}$
10. $6\frac{1}{3}$ ◯ $7\frac{1}{2}$
11. 4.2 ◯ 2.4
12. 3.1 ◯ 3.0

13. $\frac{4}{7}$ ◯ $\frac{6}{7}$
14. $\frac{9}{8}$ ◯ $\frac{13}{8}$
15. 0.05 ◯ 0.03
16. 0.2 ◯ 0.3

Add or subtract.

17. $\frac{2}{9} + \frac{5}{9} =$ _____
18. $\frac{4}{5} - \frac{1}{5} =$ _____
19. $2\frac{2}{3} + 1\frac{2}{3} =$ _____

20. 4.2
    -1.3

21. $5\frac{1}{7}$
    $-2\frac{5}{7}$

22. 21.43
    -8.65

23. $8\frac{4}{9}$
    $-3\frac{7}{9}$

24. $6\frac{2}{5}$
    $-1\frac{4}{5}$

25. $5\frac{1}{3}$
    $-3\frac{2}{3}$

26. $3\frac{4}{7}$
    $-2\frac{5}{7}$

27. 16.15
    -7.68

Solve.

28. A carpenter has a block of wood 2.4 meters long. He cuts off 1.8 meters. How long is the block of wood now?

_____

UNIT 3 LESSON 6 — Comparing, Adding, and Subtracting with the Same Unit **61**

3-6 Remembering

1 Sarah can read 4 pages in 20 minutes. If she continues to read at the same rate, how many minutes will it take Sarah to read 7 pages?

_____

2 Plot these ordered pairs: A(4, 2), B(1, 6), C(7, 6). Plot point D and draw segments to form parallelogram ABCD. Segment AB is 5 units long. Find the perimeter and area of parallelogram ABCD

P = _____

A = _____

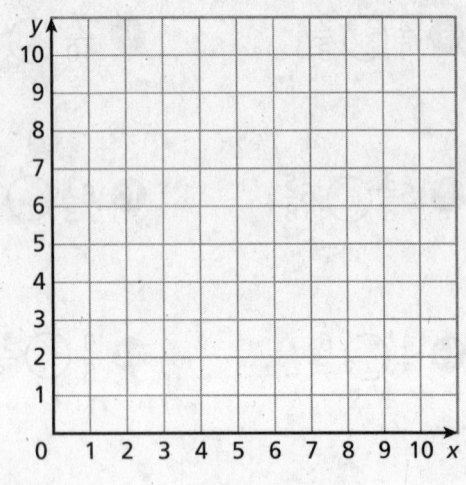

For each problem, write if you need to *multiply* or *divide*. Then solve.

3 Maria bought 5.5 pounds of pork for $13.75. How much was the cost of the pork per pound?

_____

4 Jeremiah ran 5.6 miles every day for 2 weeks. How many miles did he run in all?

_____

5 A chalkboard has an area of 35.8 square feet. A smaller chalkboard is 0.7 times that size. What is the area of the smaller chalkboard?

_____

6 Han's garden has an area of 193.75 square feet. If the length of the garden is 12.5 feet, what is the width?

_____

7 Stretch Your Thinking Kendra, John, and Angel go to the same school. John lives 0.8 times as far as Kendra does from the school. Angel lives 1.3 times as far as Kendra. If Angel lives 5.59 miles from school, how far do Kendra and John live from school?

_____

3-7 Homework

Complete each statement with < or >.

1) 0.2 ◯ 0.04   2) 1.02 ◯ 1.2   3) 0.35 ◯ 0.3

4) $\frac{4}{5}$ ◯ $\frac{11}{20}$ 5) $\frac{5}{24}$ ◯ $\frac{3}{8}$ 6) $\frac{1}{4}$ ◯ $\frac{5}{16}$

Add.

7) $\frac{1}{3} + \frac{1}{6} =$ _____   8) $\frac{1}{16} + \frac{5}{8} =$ _____   9) $0.2 + 0.08 =$ _____

10) $2.31 + 0.4 =$ _____   11) $\frac{5}{12} + \frac{3}{4} =$ _____   12) $0.19 + 0.9 =$ _____

13) $\frac{8}{9} + \frac{1}{3} =$ _____   14) $\frac{1}{5} + \frac{3}{20} =$ _____   15) $0.91 + 0.1 =$ _____

Subtract.

16) $\frac{1}{2} - \frac{1}{6} =$ _____   17) $\frac{11}{12} - \frac{5}{6} =$ _____   18) $0.4 - 0.18 =$ _____

19) $4.35 - 0.6 =$ _____   20) $\frac{10}{24} - \frac{3}{8} =$ _____   21) $0.19 - 0.1 =$ _____

22) $2.15 - 1.4 =$ _____   23) $\frac{4}{5} - \frac{5}{15} =$ _____   24) $\frac{23}{24} - \frac{5}{6} =$ _____

Solve.   *Show your work.*

25) A bush is 2.3 meters tall. It is growing next to a fence that is 3.2 meters tall. How much shorter than the fence is the bush?

_____

26) Lori had $\frac{3}{8}$ of a bag of flour for a recipe. Her friend gave her $\frac{1}{4}$ of a bag. How much flour does Lori have?

_____

27) Leroy spent $\frac{5}{9}$ of the study period working on math. Marta spent $\frac{1}{3}$ of the study period working on math. How much more of the period did Leroy work on math than Marta?

_____

UNIT 3 LESSON 7   Equivalent Fractions or Decimals   **63**

3-7 Remembering

1 Shaina and her little brother Shaud are making friendship bracelets. For every 8 bracelets Shaina makes, Shaud makes 5 bracelets. If the ratio stays the same, how many bracelets will Shaud make if Shaina makes 32 bracelets?

_____

2 Gerrard is a painter. He is using a canvas that is in the shape of a regular hexagon. The perimeter of the canvas is 78 in. The perpendicular distance from a side to the center is 11 in. to the nearest inch. Based on these measurements, what is area of the canvas?

_____

For each problem, write if you need to *multiply* or *divide*. Then solve.

3 Stephen is buying storage boxes for a card game. Each box holds 75 cards. If he has 235 cards, how many storage boxes does he need to hold all the cards?

_____

4 Isabella has $15.57 to buy strawberries at the store. Each pint of strawberries costs $2.35. How many full pints of strawberries can Isabella buy?

_____

5 The Van Ness family is playing games. They decide to spend 0.75 hour playing each of 5 games. For how long will the family play games?

_____

6 Jordan has a board that is 56.4 cm long. He cuts the board into 12 equal pieces. How long is each piece?

_____

7 Stretch Your Thinking Genna, Tasmina, and Juan participated in a long jumping competition. Their jump lengths were $2\frac{2}{5}$ meters, $3\frac{1}{3}$ meters, and $2\frac{2}{7}$ meters. Genna had the longest jump. Juan's jump was not the shortest. How far did each student jump?

_____

64 UNIT 3 LESSON 7   Equivalent Fractions or Decimals

3-8 Homework

Complete each statement with < or >.

1. $\frac{5}{8}$ ◯ $\frac{7}{10}$

2. $\frac{1}{4}$ ◯ $\frac{3}{10}$

3. $\frac{2}{3}$ ◯ $\frac{5}{7}$

4. $\frac{5}{6}$ ◯ $\frac{7}{10}$

Add or subtract.

5. $\frac{3}{8} + \frac{5}{12} =$ _____

6. $\frac{1}{3} + \frac{5}{8} =$ _____

7. $2\frac{6}{7} + 4\frac{4}{5} =$ _____

8. $3\frac{5}{6} + 2\frac{3}{5} =$ _____

9. $5\frac{3}{4} - 3\frac{5}{6} =$ _____

10. $4\frac{1}{2} - 2\frac{8}{9} =$ _____

11. $3\frac{5}{8} - 1\frac{5}{6} =$ _____

12. $5\frac{1}{3} - 2\frac{4}{5} =$ _____

Solve. *Show your work.*

13. Linda bought $2\frac{2}{3}$ yards of fabric for a project. She used $1\frac{1}{4}$ yards. How much fabric does she have left?

_____

14. Jerry rides his bike $1\frac{3}{10}$ miles one day. He bikes $1\frac{5}{8}$ miles the next day. How far does he ride in the two days altogether?

_____

UNIT 3 LESSON 8 — Finding a Common Unit Fraction **65**

3-8 Remembering

1 The table shows the prices of dog treats. If Michelle spends $24 on 9 boxes of treats, which treats does she buy?

Tasty Bits	2 boxes for $3
Crispy Treats	3 boxes for $8
Doggie Strips	1 box for $2

2 Mr. Beni sketched this floor plan of several rooms in his house. How much carpeting does Mr. Beni need to cover all of the floor space shown?

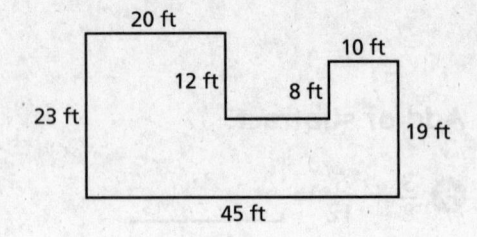

Complete each statement with < or >.

3 $\frac{4}{5} \bigcirc \frac{4}{7}$ **4** $\frac{3}{8} \bigcirc \frac{5}{16}$ **5** $0.7 \bigcirc 0.9$ **6** $\frac{7}{24} \bigcirc \frac{1}{4}$

7 $\frac{4}{9} \bigcirc \frac{2}{3}$ **8** $1.03 \bigcirc 1.3$ **9** $0.76 \bigcirc 0.7$ **10** $\frac{5}{9} \bigcirc \frac{2}{9}$

Add or subtract.

11 45.7
-8.9

12 $8\frac{1}{3}$
$-6\frac{2}{3}$

13 5.6
$+1.9$

14 $\frac{9}{10}$
$-\frac{2}{5}$

15 $\frac{15}{16}$
$-\frac{5}{8}$

16 23.8
-17.8

17 16.3
-7.6

18 $3\frac{6}{7}$
$+1\frac{3}{7}$

19 Stretch Your Thinking Cheryl goes shopping with a gift card. She spends $4.50 on a belt. Then she spends $21.75 on a necklace. She has $25.60 left on the gift card. How much was on the gift card when she started shopping?

3-9 Homework   Name _____   Date _____

Add or subtract.

① $1.32 + 2.8 = $ _____

② $9\frac{1}{2} - 5\frac{2}{3} = $ _____

③ $3\frac{1}{4} - 1\frac{11}{12} = $ _____

④ $\frac{2}{3} + 1\frac{5}{7} = $ _____

⑤ $2.7 - 0.82 = $ _____

⑥ $4\frac{3}{8} + 2\frac{3}{10} = $ _____

⑦ $\frac{6}{11} - \frac{1}{5} = $ _____

⑧ $5.13 + 2.8 = $ _____

⑨ $1\frac{4}{5} + \frac{3}{10} = $ _____

⑩ $2\frac{1}{2} - \frac{3}{8} = $ _____

⑪ $2.18 - 1.3 = $ _____

⑫ $2\frac{3}{4} + 5\frac{7}{10} = $ _____

Complete each statement with < or >.

⑬ $1.8 \bigcirc 1.08$

⑭ $\frac{2}{3} \bigcirc \frac{3}{5}$

⑮ $1\frac{7}{12} \bigcirc 1\frac{5}{8}$

⑯ $3\frac{2}{3} \bigcirc 3\frac{8}{9}$

⑰ $0.14 \bigcirc 0.41$

⑱ $\frac{2}{5} \bigcirc \frac{1}{10}$

UNIT 3 LESSON 9   Mixed Problem Solving

3-9 Remembering

1. Hannah is helping her father install a patio. For every 12 square bricks, they are using 10 round bricks. If they use 35 round bricks, how many square bricks will they use?

_____

2. Jerry is painting the shaded part of this banner. What is the area of the part of the banner he is painting?

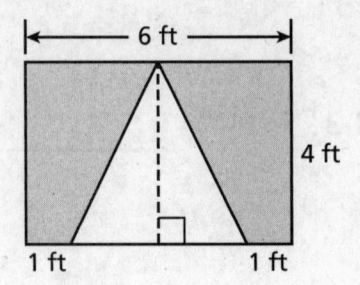

_____

Complete each statement with < or >.

3. $\frac{1}{2} \bigcirc \frac{5}{8}$

4. $\frac{4}{5} \bigcirc \frac{5}{7}$

5. $0.33 \bigcirc 0.41$

6. $\frac{3}{5} \bigcirc \frac{5}{8}$

7. $6.07 \bigcirc 6.17$

8. $\frac{1}{6} \bigcirc \frac{3}{10}$

9. $\frac{5}{8} \bigcirc \frac{7}{12}$

10. $11.29 \bigcirc 11.31$

Add or subtract.

11. $\frac{4}{5} + \frac{1}{8}$

12. $2\frac{2}{3} - 1\frac{1}{3}$

13. $27.1 + 12.6$

14. $\frac{1}{2} + \frac{3}{8}$

15. $2\frac{3}{7} - 1\frac{2}{3}$

16. $4.45 + 14.6 =$ _____

17. $5\frac{1}{2} + 1\frac{8}{9}$

18. $10.04 + 8.2 =$ _____

19. **Stretch Your Thinking** Lucy has $3\frac{3}{4}$ feet of ribbon. She needs $1\frac{1}{2}$ feet of ribbon for one project. She needs $1\frac{5}{6}$ feet of ribbon for another project. Will Lucy have more or less than $\frac{1}{2}$ foot of ribbon left after she completes both projects? Explain.

_____

_____

3-10 Homework

Multiply.

1. $\frac{3}{8} \cdot 10 = $ _____

2. $\frac{7}{8} \cdot 11 = $ _____

3. $\frac{4}{5} \cdot 12 = $ _____

4. $9 \cdot \frac{2}{3} = $ _____

5. $10 \cdot \frac{5}{7} = $ _____

6. $2 \cdot \frac{3}{5} = $ _____

7. $\frac{2}{3} \cdot \frac{6}{7} = $ _____

8. $\frac{5}{8} \cdot \frac{1}{3} = $ _____

9. $\frac{4}{7} \cdot \frac{5}{7} = $ _____

10. $1\frac{2}{9} \cdot 2\frac{1}{3} = $ _____

11. $2\frac{4}{5} \cdot 3\frac{1}{8} = $ _____

12. $4\frac{1}{6} \cdot 2\frac{2}{5} = $ _____

Dear Math Students,

This summer, I am going to earn money mowing lawns. I can mow $\frac{2}{3}$ of a lawn in 1 hour. My friend told me that if I work for 5 hours, I can multiply $5 \cdot \frac{2}{3}$ to find the number of lawns I've mowed. But I said that in 5 hours, I'd mow $\frac{2}{15}$ of a lawn. Does my answer seem reasonable?

Your friend,
Puzzled Penguin

13. Write a response to Puzzled Penguin.

_____

_____

UNIT 3 LESSON 10 — Multiplying with Fractions

3-10 Remembering

1 During a storm, snow fell 4 inches every 2 hours. At this rate, how long will it take for 10 inches of snow to fall?

_____

Find the perimeter and area of each figure.

2 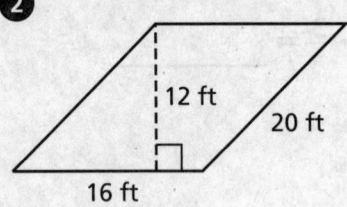 Parallelogram with height 12 ft, slant side 20 ft, base 16 ft.

P = _____
A = _____

3 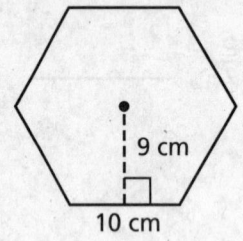 Hexagon with apothem 9 cm and side 10 cm.

P = _____
A = _____

4 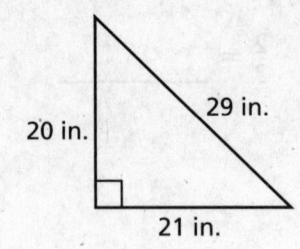 Right triangle with legs 20 in. and 21 in., hypotenuse 29 in.

P = _____
A = _____

Complete each statement with < or >.

5 $\frac{3}{4}$ ◯ $\frac{6}{7}$ **6** $\frac{1}{3}$ ◯ $\frac{1}{5}$ **7** 9.03 ◯ 9.1   **8** 4.56 ◯ 5.01

Add or subtract.

9 $\frac{5}{6} - \frac{1}{2}$

10 $1\frac{4}{5} - \frac{4}{9}$

11 133.9 + 29.9

12 $\frac{3}{8} + \frac{1}{3}$

13 $3\frac{1}{4} - 1\frac{2}{3}$

14 44.9 + 2.3

15 14.22 + 20.1

16 5.99 − 1.08

17 Stretch Your Thinking Marty has a box of raisins. He uses $1\frac{1}{2}$ cups of raisins for trail mix. Then he opens a bag with $2\frac{1}{3}$ cups of raisins in it. Marty then uses $\frac{3}{4}$ cup of raisins for bread pudding. There are $3\frac{1}{2}$ cups of raisins left. How many cups of raisins were in the box? Explain.

_____

_____

_____

3-11 Homework Name _____ Date _____

Divide.

① $\frac{1}{2} \div 3 =$ _____

② $12 \div \frac{1}{6} =$ _____

③ $8 \div 7 =$ _____

④ $10 \div \frac{1}{4} =$ _____

⑤ $14 \div \frac{1}{3} =$ _____

⑥ $\frac{1}{6} \div 3 =$ _____

⑦ $\frac{1}{12} \div 8 =$ _____

⑧ $9 \div 14 =$ _____

⑨ $\frac{1}{8} \div 4 =$ _____

⑩ $10 \div 11 =$ _____

⑪ $13 \div 12 =$ _____

⑫ $\frac{1}{3} \div 7 =$ _____

⑬ $9 \div \frac{1}{4} =$ _____

⑭ $11 \div 6 =$ _____

⑮ $\frac{1}{5} \div 14 =$ _____

⑯ Kim ran 4 blocks in the time it took her little brother Mikey to toddle $\frac{1}{3}$ block.

   a. Kim ran how many times as many blocks as Mikey toddled? Explain how you found your answer.
   _____
   _____

   b. Mikey toddled how many times as many blocks as Kim ran? Explain how you found your answer.
   _____
   _____

UNIT 3 LESSON 11 Dividing with Fractions and Whole Numbers 71

3-11 Remembering

1 On the sixth grade field trip, there are 2 teachers for every 9 students. If there are 63 students on the trip, how many teachers are there?

_____

Find the unknown side length.

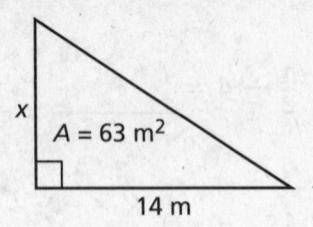

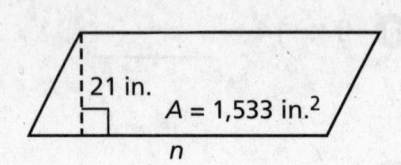

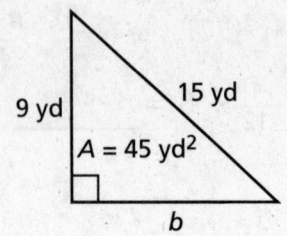

2 Triangle with x, A = 63 m², and base 14 m.

x = _____

3 Parallelogram with height 21 in., A = 1,533 in.², base n.

n = _____

4 Triangle with sides 9 yd, 15 yd, A = 45 yd², base b.

b = _____

Add or subtract.

5 $1\frac{2}{3}$
$+ 3\frac{4}{5}$

6 $\frac{7}{10}$
$- \frac{4}{10}$

7 105.7
 + 16.9

8 23.9
 − 9.1

Multiply.

9 $\frac{5}{6} \cdot \frac{1}{4} = $ _____

10 $\frac{3}{10} \cdot \frac{4}{9} = $ _____

11 $\frac{5}{7} \cdot \frac{5}{6} = $ _____

12 $\frac{2}{3} \cdot \frac{9}{14} = $ _____

13 $1\frac{2}{3} \cdot 2\frac{1}{3} = $ _____

14 $3\frac{4}{5} \cdot 1\frac{1}{2} = $ _____

15 $2\frac{4}{5} \cdot 2\frac{3}{4} = $ _____

16 $1\frac{4}{5} \cdot \frac{3}{10} = $ _____

17 Stretch Your Thinking Joelle's cooking class is $2\frac{1}{2}$ times as long as her karate class. Her cooking class starts at 4 P.M. If her karate class is $\frac{1}{2}$ hour long, at what time does her cooking class end? Explain.

_____

_____

_____

3-12 Homework

Multiplying a number by a fraction less than 1 results in a lesser number. Dividing a number by a fraction less than 1 results in a greater number.

Multiply or divide.

1) $12 \div 13 =$ _____

2) $8 \div \frac{1}{2} =$ _____

3) $\frac{1}{2} \div 8 =$ _____

4) $\frac{2}{5} \cdot \frac{3}{8} =$ _____

5) $14 \div \frac{1}{3} =$ _____

6) $\frac{1}{5} \div 10 =$ _____

7) $1\frac{1}{3} \cdot 2\frac{1}{4} =$ _____

8) $\frac{3}{5} \cdot 6 =$ _____

9) $30 \div \frac{1}{3} =$ _____

10) $1\frac{2}{3} \cdot \frac{7}{10} =$ _____

11) $\frac{11}{15} \cdot \frac{5}{6} =$ _____

12) $\frac{1}{8} \div 7 =$ _____

13) $15 \div 8 =$ _____

14) $24 \div \frac{1}{3} =$ _____

15) $\frac{5}{8} \cdot \frac{4}{25} =$ _____

16) $\frac{3}{7} \cdot \frac{2}{3} =$ _____

17) $\frac{1}{9} \div 4 =$ _____

18) $17 \div \frac{1}{2} =$ _____

Solve. *Show your work.*

19) The fire station is 9 kilometers from the library. Tracey walked $\frac{3}{5}$ of the distance. How far did Tracey walk?

20) Tony usually saves $\frac{1}{5}$ of his allowance. Last week, he only saved $\frac{2}{3}$ as much. How much of his allowance did he save last week?

21) A fabric designer is placing beaded stars on her fabric. She decides to place one star in the middle of every $\frac{1}{3}$ yard. How many beaded stars will she place on 8 yards of fabric?

UNIT 3 LESSON 12 — Is It Multiplying or Dividing? 73

3-12 Remembering

1 Sudian reads 4 pages in 12 minutes. At this rate, how long will it take him to read 6 pages?

_____

2 Fill in the missing numbers in the rate table. Then plot the ordered pairs and draw a line through the points.

Number of Pounds	Number of Dollars
1	2
2	4
3	
4	
5	

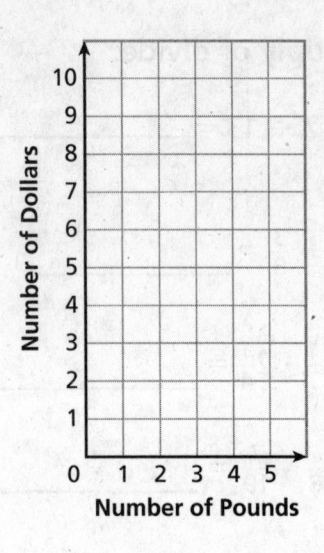

Simplify.

3 4.45 + 12.8 = _____

4 4.4 • 11.7 = _____

5 41.14 ÷ 3.4 = _____

6 $1\frac{1}{7} + 1\frac{3}{4}$ = _____

7 $2\frac{1}{2} - 1\frac{3}{4}$ = _____

8 $1\frac{5}{9} + 2\frac{1}{3}$ = _____

9 $2\frac{1}{2} \cdot 1\frac{1}{2}$ = _____

10 $\frac{2}{9} \cdot \frac{3}{10}$ = _____

11 $\frac{3}{4} \div \frac{1}{2}$ = _____

12 Stretch Your Thinking Xavier is using square tiles to cover a table top. The tiles are $1\frac{1}{2}$ in. on each side. The table top is $7\frac{1}{2}$ inches wide and $13\frac{1}{2}$ inches long. How many tiles does Xavier need to use to cover the whole table? Explain.

_____

_____

74 UNIT 3 LESSON 12   Is It Multiplying or Dividing?

3-13 Homework

Find the unknown factor in each equation. Then rewrite the multiplication as a division equation.

Multiplication Equation	Related Division Equation
① $\frac{3}{5} \cdot \boxed{} = \frac{9}{20}$	$\frac{9}{20} \div \frac{3}{5} = \boxed{}$
② $\frac{5}{6} \cdot \boxed{} = \frac{20}{42}$	
③ $\frac{4}{9} \cdot \boxed{} = \frac{24}{63}$	

Divide.

④ $\frac{8}{28} \div \frac{4}{7} = $ _____

⑤ $\frac{9}{16} \div \frac{3}{4} = $ _____

⑥ $\frac{30}{56} \div \frac{5}{8} = $ _____

⑦ $2\frac{11}{14} \div \frac{3}{7} = $ _____

The products in each multiplication equation are simplified. Find the unknown factor. Then choose a related division equation to solve. Explain your choice.

⑧ $\frac{5}{6} \cdot $ _____ $= \frac{15}{42} = \frac{5}{14}$ Solve $\frac{15}{42} \div \frac{5}{6} = $ _____ or $\frac{5}{14} \div \frac{5}{6} = $ _____

_____

Draw a diagram, write an equation, and solve.

⑨ Danielle has a canvas painting that has an area of $\frac{6}{35}$ square meters and a length of $\frac{2}{5}$ meter. What is the width of the painting?

_____

⑩ Youngshim can kick the soccer ball $\frac{8}{15}$ the length of the play yard. This is $\frac{2}{5}$ of the distance her older brother Minjun can kick the ball. Have far can Minjun kick the ball?

_____

UNIT 3 LESSON 13   Dividing Numerators and Denominators **75**

3-13 Remembering

1. There are 15 pieces in 3 building sets. How many pieces are there in 8 building sets?

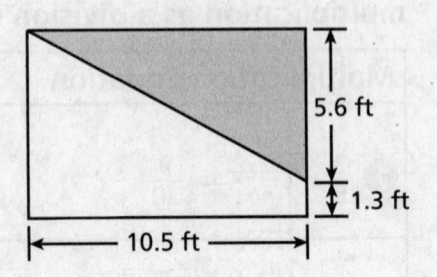

_____

2. The unshaded part shows the area of Milia's garden. What is the area of Milia's garden?

_____

(Figure: rectangle 10.5 ft wide, with heights 5.6 ft and 1.3 ft; a diagonal line creates a shaded triangle in the upper right.)

Write equivalent fractions. Then compare, add, and multiply the fractions from left to right. Subtract the lesser fraction from the greater fraction.

3	$\frac{7}{8}$	$\frac{5}{6}$	→	
4	>, <			
5	+			
6	·			
7	−			

8	$\frac{3}{5}$	$\frac{1}{4}$	→	
9	>, <			
10	+			
11	·			
12	−			

13	$\frac{5}{8}$	$\frac{7}{10}$	→	
14	>, <			
15	+			
16	·			
17	−			

18. Sam read 6 books in the time it took his little sister, Faith, to read $\frac{1}{2}$ of a book.

  a. Sam read how many times as many books as his sister read? Explain how you found your answer.

  _____

  b. Sam's sister read how many times as many books as Sam read? Explain how you found your answer.

  _____

19. Stretch Your Thinking The difference between two numbers is 5. One number is $\frac{2}{3}$ the other number. What are the two numbers? Explain how you got your answer.

_____

_____

UNIT 3 LESSON 13 — Dividing Numerators and Denominators

3-14 Homework

Divide by unsimplifying and dividing numerators and denominators or by multiplying by the reciprocal.

1) $\frac{9}{20} \div \frac{3}{5} =$ _____

2) $\frac{5}{7} \div \frac{6}{11} =$ _____

3) $\frac{2}{3} \div \frac{4}{7} =$ _____

4) $\frac{7}{20} \div \frac{7}{5} =$ _____

5) $\frac{8}{9} \div \frac{2}{3} =$ _____

6) $\frac{2}{5} \div \frac{3}{7} =$ _____

7) $4\frac{2}{5} \div \frac{6}{7} =$ _____

8) $6\frac{3}{10} \div \frac{9}{5} =$ _____

The problems below are solved by unsimplifying and dividing and by multiplying by the reciprocal. Complete the solutions.

9) **Unsimplify and Divide** Notice that the denominators divide. You need to unsimplify to be able to divide the numerators.

$$\frac{7}{15} \div \frac{2}{5} = \frac{7}{15} \cdot \frac{\square}{\square} \div \frac{2}{5} = \frac{7 \cdot \square}{15 \cdot \square} \div \frac{2}{5} = \frac{7}{3} \cdot \frac{1}{2} = \frac{\square}{\square}$$

with $\_\_ \div 2 = 1$ and $15 \div 5 = 3$

Multiply by the Reciprocal of the Divisor

$$\frac{7}{15} \div \frac{2}{5} = \frac{7}{15} \cdot \frac{\square}{\square} = _____$$

10) **Unsimplify and Divide** Notice that the numerators divide. You need to unsimplify to be able to divide the denominators.

$$\frac{21}{8} \div \frac{7}{5} = \left(\frac{21}{8} \cdot \frac{\square}{\square}\right) \div \frac{7}{5} = \frac{21 \cdot \square}{8 \cdot \square} \div \frac{7}{5} = \frac{3}{8} \cdot \frac{5}{1} = \frac{\square}{\square}$$

with $21 \div 7 = 3$ and $\_\_ \div 5 = 1$

Multiply by the Reciprocal of the Divisor

$$\frac{21}{8} \div \frac{7}{5} = \frac{21}{8} \cdot \frac{\square}{\square} = _____$$

UNIT 3 LESSON 14 — Dividing by Unsimplifying

3-14 Remembering

1 Drake and Troy are building models. For every 10 pieces Drake puts together, Troy puts together 6 pieces. If Troy puts together 18 pieces, how many pieces does Drake put together?

_____

Divide.

2 $23\overline{)56.58}$ **3** $5.4\overline{)187.92}$ **4** $6\overline{)612}$ **5** $8\overline{)49.76}$

Find the unknown factor in each question. Then rewrite the multiplication as a division equation.

6 $\dfrac{8}{9} \cdot \dfrac{\square}{\square} = \dfrac{24}{36}$

7 $\dfrac{5}{11} \cdot \dfrac{\square}{\square} = \dfrac{25}{66}$

8 $\dfrac{2}{7} \cdot \dfrac{\square}{\square} = \dfrac{10}{49}$

9 $\dfrac{7}{20} \cdot \dfrac{\square}{\square} = \dfrac{21}{100}$

10 Stretch Your Thinking Ginny went to the store with a gift card. She spent $\dfrac{2}{5}$ of the amount on her gift card. Then she spent $15 more of the money on the card. Her mom gave her $25 in cash. Then she spent $\dfrac{1}{2}$ of the total amount she had. She had a total of $14 left to spend. How much was on Ginny's gift card? Explain your answer.

_____

_____

_____

3-15 Homework

Divide using any method.

1. $\frac{7}{9} \div \frac{4}{9} =$ _____

2. $\frac{1}{18} \div \frac{1}{6} =$ _____

3. $\frac{5}{6} \div \frac{2}{3} =$ _____

4. $\frac{5}{6} \div 7 =$ _____

5. $4 \div \frac{1}{12} =$ _____

6. $4 \div \frac{5}{12} =$ _____

7. $\frac{9}{16} \div \frac{3}{8} =$ _____

8. $\frac{5}{6} \div \frac{1}{7} =$ _____

Solve.   *Show your work.*

9. Pam's cats Scooter and Max are playing with yarn. Scooter's yarn is $1\frac{2}{3}$ yards long. Max's yarn is $\frac{3}{4}$ yard long. Scooter's yarn is how many times as long as Max's?

10. Mr. Dawson divides $\frac{7}{8}$ pound of raisins between 3 batches of oatmeal muffins. What is the weight of the raisins in each batch?

11. A rabbit pen has an area of $1\frac{1}{2}$ square yards. If the length of the pen is $\frac{2}{3}$ yard, what is its width?

12. Darryl knit a scarf $\frac{3}{5}$ yard long. This is $\frac{2}{3}$ the length of the scarf Hannah knit. How long is Hannah's scarf?

UNIT 3 LESSON 15   Dividing by Multiplying by the Reciprocal

3-15 Remembering

1. To make a green paint, Michelle mixes 4 cans of blue paint with 6 cans of yellow paint. She has 24 cans of yellow paint. How many cans of blue paint does she need in order to get the same shade of green?

_____

2. Marjory is buying fence for the part of her backyard shown. How much fencing does she need to buy? Marjory is covering the area with river rocks. What area is enclosed by the fence?

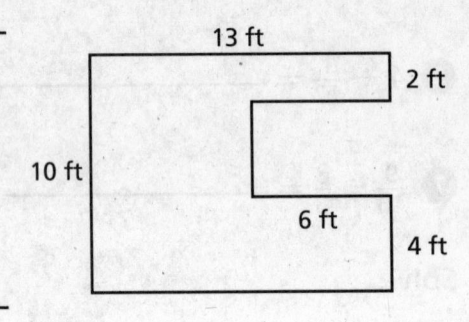

(Diagram: 13 ft, 2 ft, 10 ft, 6 ft, 4 ft)

_____

Simplify.

3. $34.9 + 13 =$ **4.** $17 - 12.8 =$ **5.** $23 \cdot 38 =$ **6.** $39.65 \div 6.1 =$

Write equivalent fractions. Then compare, add, multiply, and divide the fractions from left to right. Subtract the lesser fraction from the greater fraction.

7	$\frac{2}{5}$ $\frac{1}{3}$ →	
8	>, <	
9	+	
10	·	
11	÷	
12	−	

13	$\frac{5}{7}$ $\frac{1}{3}$ →	
14	>, <	
15	+	
16	·	
17	÷	
18	−	

19	$\frac{10}{11}$ $\frac{2}{5}$ →	
20	>, <	
21	+	
22	·	
23	÷	
24	−	

25. Stretch Your Thinking Ben saved $\frac{3}{4}$ as much each month as he saved the month before. If he saved $45 in March, how much did he save the January before?

_____
_____

Dividing by Multiplying by the Reciprocal

3-16 Homework   Name _____   Date _____

Will each product or quotient below be greater or less than the first fraction? Circle your prediction, and then find the actual product or quotient to check your prediction.

1 $\frac{4}{5} \div \frac{5}{6}$ Predict: $> \frac{4}{5}$ or $< \frac{4}{5}$

$\frac{4}{5} \div \frac{5}{6} =$ _____

2 $\frac{2}{9} \cdot \frac{3}{4}$ Predict: $> \frac{2}{9}$ or $< \frac{2}{9}$

$\frac{2}{9} \cdot \frac{3}{4} =$ _____

3 $1\frac{3}{4} \cdot \frac{4}{7}$ Predict: $> 1\frac{3}{4}$ or $< 1\frac{3}{4}$

$1\frac{3}{4} \cdot \frac{4}{7} =$ _____

4 $\frac{1}{8} \div \frac{1}{10}$ Predict: $> \frac{1}{8}$ or $< \frac{1}{8}$

$\frac{1}{8} \div \frac{1}{10} =$ _____

Decide if you need to multiply or divide. Then solve.

5 A pitcher contains $1\frac{5}{8}$ quarts of orange juice. How many full cups, each having a $\frac{1}{4}$-quart capacity, can be filled from the pitcher?

_____

6 A bread recipe calls for $1\frac{1}{4}$ cups of wheat flour. A muffin recipe calls for $1\frac{1}{5}$ times this much. How much wheat flour is needed for the muffin recipe?

_____

7 The base (b) of a rectangle is $2\frac{1}{4}$ inches and its height (h) is $1\frac{3}{8}$ inches. What is the area of the rectangle?

_____

8 A parallelogram has an area (A) of $24\frac{4}{5}$ cm² and a height (h) of 8 cm. Use the formula $A = bh$ to find the base measure (b) of the parallelogram.

_____

3-16 Remembering

1 It takes the Cosway family 3 hours to play 5 games. At that rate, how many games could the family play in 9 hours?

_____

2 Mr. Carbone is painting part of a wall as shown. Each can of paint covers 20 square feet. How many cans of paint does he need to cover the wall?

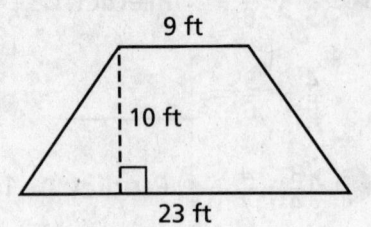

_____

(Trapezoid with top 9 ft, height 10 ft, bottom 23 ft)

Write equivalent fractions. Then compare, add, multiply, and divide the fractions from left to right. Subtract the lesser fraction from the greater fraction.

3	$\frac{2}{9}$ $\frac{1}{3}$ →	
4	>, <	
5	+	
6	·	
7	÷	
8	−	

9	$\frac{1}{4}$ $\frac{7}{10}$ →	
10	>, <	
11	+	
12	·	
13	÷	
14	−	

15	$\frac{5}{7}$ $\frac{3}{5}$ →	
16	>, <	
17	+	
18	·	
19	÷	
20	−	

21 Joseph cuts a board that is 3.8 feet long. Justine cuts a board that is 0.5 times as long as Joseph's. How long is Justine's board?

_____

22 **Stretch Your Thinking** The area of the floor in Hanna's room is $99\frac{3}{7}$ square feet. The area of her kitchen is $1\frac{3}{4}$ the area of her room. If the length of her kitchen is $14\frac{1}{2}$ feet, how wide is the kitchen? Explain how you got your answer.

_____

_____

82 UNIT 3 LESSON 16   Is It Multiplying or Dividing?

3-17 Homework

Solve.
Show your work.

1 A large bag of apples weighs $5\frac{1}{2}$ pounds, which is $2\frac{3}{4}$ pounds more than a small bag of apples. What is the weight of a small bag of apples?

_____

2 Four identical plastic containers are each filled with wheat germ. The total weight of the four containers is $\frac{5}{8}$ pound. What is the weight of each container?

_____

3 Tim earned $123 for working $7\frac{1}{2}$ hours on Saturday. What amount does Tim earn per hour?

_____

4 At the beginning of a science experiment, the temperature of a mixture was 19.62°C. At the end of the experiment, the temperature was 81.9°C. By what number of degrees did the temperature increase?

_____

Simplify.

5 $\frac{3}{10} \div \frac{1}{5} =$ _____

6 $\frac{11}{14} - \frac{3}{7} =$ _____

7 $\frac{7}{8} \cdot \frac{6}{7} =$ _____

8 $\frac{4}{5} \cdot \frac{5}{8} =$ _____

9 $\frac{1}{2} + \frac{2}{3} =$ _____

10 $6 - 3\frac{3}{4} =$ _____

11 $1.4 \cdot 7 =$ _____

12 $24.8 \div 0.8 =$ _____

13 $3.85 + 2.6 =$ _____

14 $5.4 \cdot 7.5 =$ _____

15 $8.1 \div 9 =$ _____

16 $2 - 1.38 =$ _____

UNIT 3 LESSON 17 — Mixed Practice with Decimals and Fractions

3-17 Remembering

1 Brendan uses 6 apples and 8 pears to make a fruit salad. If he wants the salad to taste the same, how many pears should he use if he uses 15 apples?

_____

Multiply or divide.

2 97)582

3 45 × 54

4 10.8 × 4.3

5 68)353.6

Write equivalent fractions. Then compare, add, multiply, and divide the fractions from left to right. Subtract the lesser fraction from the greater fraction.

6	$\frac{5}{6}$ $1\frac{1}{6}$ →	
7	>, <	
8	+	
9	·	
10	÷	
11	−	

12	$\frac{4}{5}$ $\frac{11}{25}$ →	
13	>, <	
14	+	
15	·	
16	÷	
17	−	

18	$1\frac{1}{4}$ $1\frac{2}{5}$ →	
19	>, <	
20	+	
21	·	
22	÷	
23	−	

Solve.

24 Stretch Your Thinking Ryan keeps his hamster cage on his dresser. The area of the top of Ryan's dresser is $1\frac{2}{3}$ as large as the area of the bottom of his hamster cage. The area of the dresser top is 960 square inches. How many square inches of his dresser top are not covered by the hamster cage? Explain how you got your answer.

_____
_____
_____

3-18 Homework

Name _____ **Date** _____

1 Choose a stock from the listings in a newspaper or from an Internet search. Write the name of the company you choose, and the most recent price for a share of the company's stock.

_____

2 Suppose you purchase 250 shares of the company's stock. Calculate the cost of your purchase.

_____

3 Record the price of one share of the stock you purchased in the *Day 1* column of the table below. Then, each day for the next four business days, find that day's price and record it in the table.

Company Name	Day 1 Price	Day 2 Price	Day 3 Price	Day 4 Price	Day 5 Price

4 Calculate the change in price. Write whether the change is an *increase* or a *decrease*.

a. from Day 1 to Day 2 _____

b. from Day 2 to Day 3 _____

c. from Day 3 to Day 4 _____

d. from Day 4 to Day 5 _____

5 Did the price per share increase or decrease over the five-day period? By what amount did it increase or decrease?

_____

6 Suppose you sell your shares at the end of the five days. Write the price per share at that time, and calculate the amount of money you should receive for selling 250 shares. Did you earn a profit, or lose money?

_____

UNIT 3 LESSON 18   Focus on Mathematical Practices

3-18 Remembering

1 It takes 4 pitchers of juice to fill 12 cups. How many pitchers does it take to fill 18 cups?

_____

2 The diagram represents a township. The town council is planning a nature preserve in the portion of the township that is not shaded. What is the planned area of the preserve?

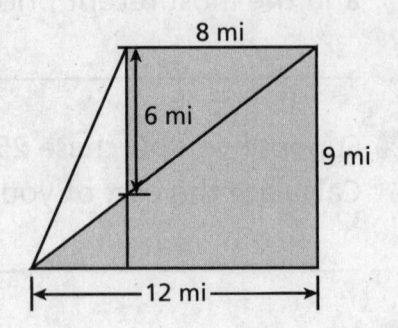

_____

Write equivalent fractions. Then compare, add, multiply, and divide the fractions from left to right. Subtract the lesser fraction from the greater fraction.

3	$\frac{3}{4}$ $\frac{2}{5}$ →	
4	>, <	
5	+	
6	·	
7	÷	
8	−	

9	$\frac{7}{9}$ $\frac{4}{5}$ →	
10	>, <	
11	+	
12	·	
13	÷	
14	−	

15	$\frac{1}{4}$ $\frac{3}{8}$ →	
16	>, <	
17	+	
18	·	
19	÷	
20	−	

Solve.

21 Jeff ran 3.25 miles. Trish ran 5.85 miles. How many times Jeff's distance did Trisha run?

_____

22 Linda bicycled 1.3 miles. If she bicycles 3.8 more miles, she will arrive at the store. How many miles is it to the store?

_____

23 Stretch Your Thinking Baily's necklace has $\frac{2}{3}$ the number of beads as Jerry's necklace. Julie's necklace has $1\frac{3}{5}$ the number of beads as Baily's necklace. If Baily's necklace has 40 beads, whose necklace has the most beads? Explain your answer.

_____

4-1 Homework

Find the surface area.

1. 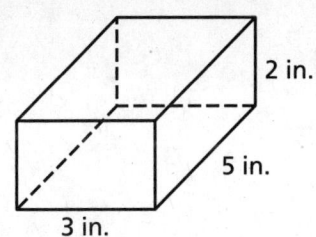 3 in. × 5 in. × 2 in.

_____

2. 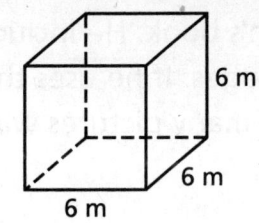 6 m × 6 m × 6 m

_____

3. 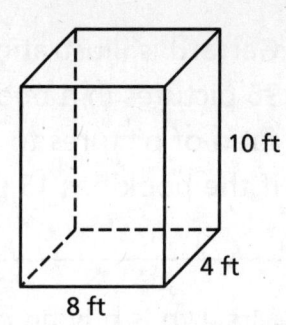 8 ft × 4 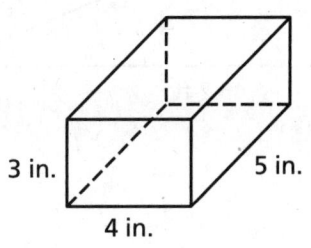 ft × 10 ft

_____

4. 4 in. × 3 in. × 5 in.

_____

5. 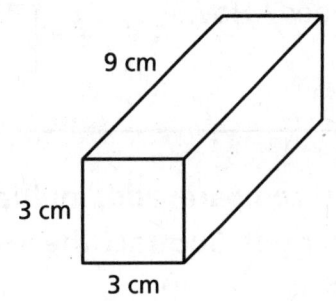 3 cm × 3 cm × 9 cm

_____

6. 3 yd × 4 yd × 2 yd

_____

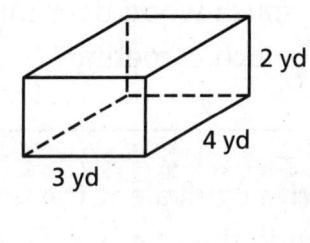

Solve.

Show your work.

7. All the faces of an antique candle box in the shape of a rectangular prism have been painted. The candle box has a length of 25 in., a width of 10 in., and a height of 8 in. What is the total area that was painted?

_____

8. Cara made a sewing box in the shape of a rectangular prism. Its length is 14 in., its width is 8 in., and its height is 6 in. Cara plans to cover the box with fabric. The fabric comes in 14 in. squares. How many squares does she need to cover all the faces with no overlap?

_____

UNIT 4 LESSON 1   Nets and Surface Area for Rectangular Prisms **87**

4-1 Remembering

Name _____ Date _____

Solve.

1 Gerrard is illustrating a children's book. He includes 36 pictures in a book with 45 pages. If he uses the same ratio of pictures to pages, how many pictures will he include if the book has 15 pages?

_____

2 Mrs. Lyn is buying wood for a baseboard in the room shown. Then she is going to install wall-to-wall carpeting. How much wood does Mrs. Lyn need? How much carpeting?

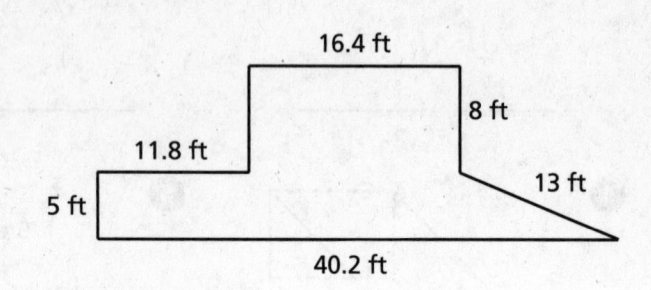

(Figure: room shape with measurements 16.4 ft, 8 ft, 11.8 ft, 13 ft, 5 ft, 40.2 ft)

_____

Write equivalent fractions. Then compare, add, multiply, and divide the numbers from left to right. Subtract the lesser number from the greater number.

3	$\frac{5}{9}$ $\frac{3}{5}$ →	
4	>, <	
5	+	
6	·	
7	÷	
8	−	

9	$1\frac{5}{6}$ $2\frac{3}{10}$ →	
10	>, <	
11	+	
12	·	
13	÷	
14	−	

15 Stretch Your Thinking Jason is making a toy box in the shape of a rectangular prism. Jason sketches one net. Then he draws another net that has double the dimensions of the first net. How do the surface areas compare? Explain.

_____

_____

4-2 Homework

Name the prism.

1. _____

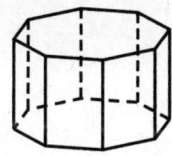

2. _____

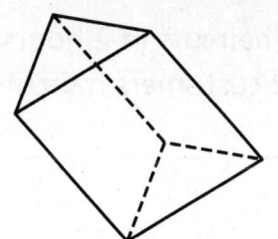

3. _____

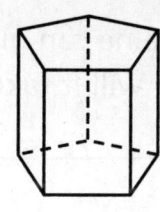

4. _____

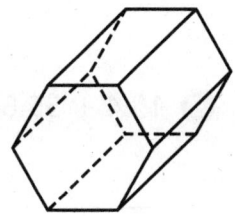

5. _____

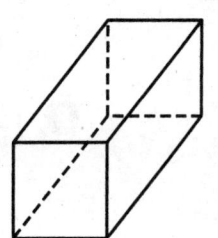

6. _____

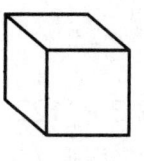

Complete.

7. Will this net form an octagonal prism? Explain.

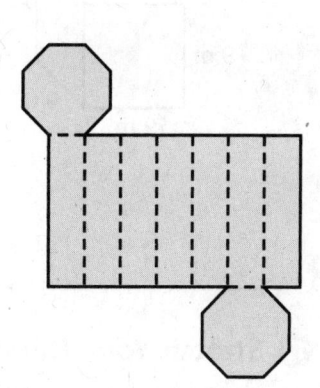

   _____

8. The base of a square prism has an area of 16 in.² The height of the prism is 6 in. What is the surface area of the square prism?

   _____

9. The perimeter of the base of a regular octagonal prism is 8 ft. What is the width of a rectangular side of the prism?

   _____

10. The base of a triangular prism has an area of 6 cm². The height of the prism is 5 cm. The width of the rectangular faces are 3 cm, 4 cm, and 5 cm. What is the surface area of the triangular prism?

    _____

UNIT 4 LESSON 2 — Nets and Surface Area for Nonrectangular Prisms **89**

4-2 Remembering

Solve.

1) Lorraine can give 3 customers haircuts in 2 hours. How long will it take her to give 12 customers haircuts?

_____

Complete.

2) $\frac{5}{6} + \frac{7}{10}$

3) $56.77 + 23.47$

4) $1.2 \cdot 22.3$

5) $1\frac{4}{5} \div \frac{2}{3}$

6) $607.3 - 122.9$

7) $1\frac{2}{9} - \frac{5}{9}$

8) $134.1 \div 3$

9) $15.4 + 55.6$

Find the surface area.

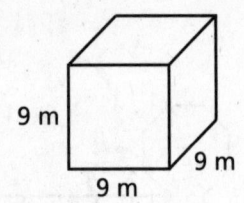

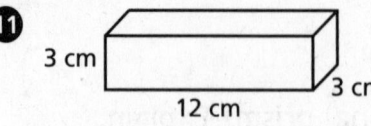

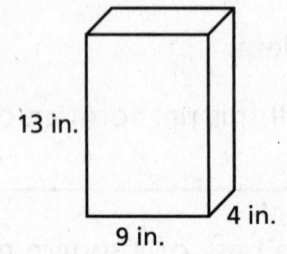

10) 9 m, 9 m, 9 m

11) 3 cm, 12 cm, 3 cm

12) 13 in., 9 in., 4 in.

13) **Stretch Your Thinking** Herga makes boxes for games that she has invented. She makes a box for one game. Then she makes a box with dimensions that are one third the dimensions of the first box. What is the relationship between the surface areas of the boxes? Explain.

_____
_____
_____

90 UNIT 4 LESSON 2 — Nets and Surface Area for Nonrectangular Prisms

4-3 Homework

Name _____ Date _____

Find the surface area.

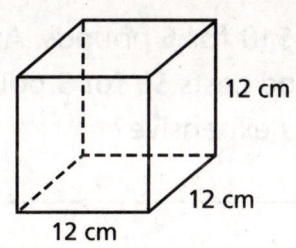

1. [rectangular prism: 8 in. × 6 in. × 4 in.]

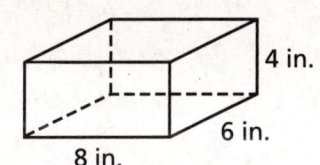

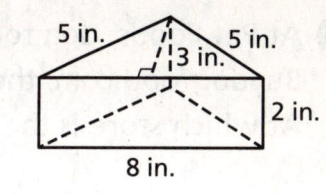

_____

2. [cube: 12 cm × 12 cm × 12 cm]

_____

3. [triangular prism: triangle sides 5 in., 5 in., base 8 in., height 3 in.; length 2 in.]

_____

4. [octagonal prism: side 4 ft, apothem 5 ft, height 8 ft]

_____

5. [pentagonal prism: side 3 ft, apothem 4 ft, height 2 ft]

_____

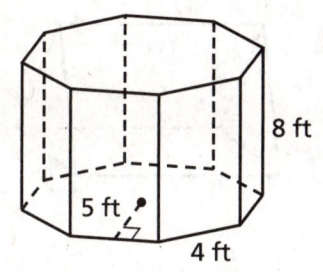

6. [hexagonal prism: side 5 in., apothem 4 in., height 4 in.]

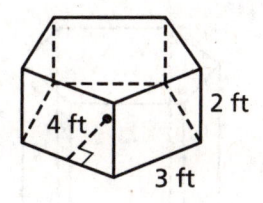

_____

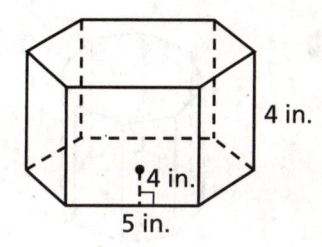

Solve.

7. Jesse bought the speakers shown at the right. All faces of the speakers except the front faces are wood. How many square inches of wood were used to make the speakers?

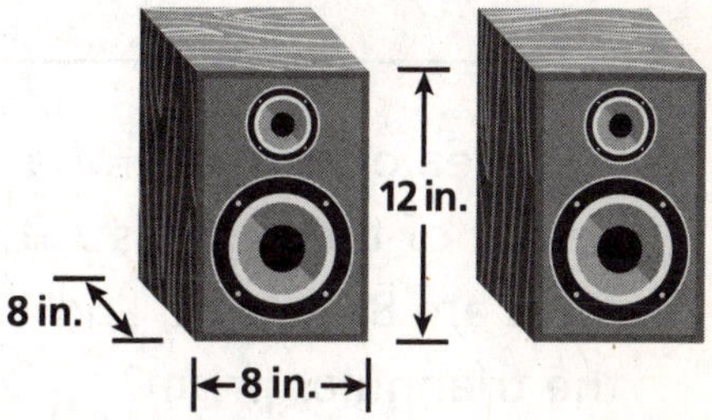

[speakers: 8 in. × 8 in. × 12 in.]

_____

8. The glass entry way to a basement store is shown at the right. How many square feet of glass were used to make the entry way?

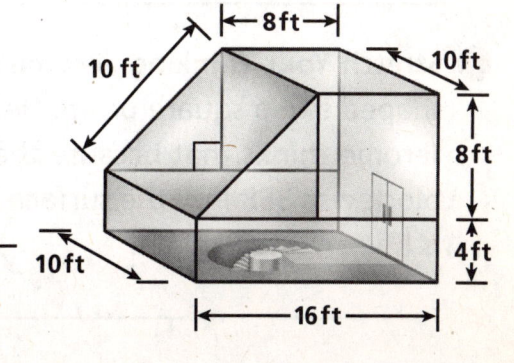

[entry way diagram: 8 ft top, 10 ft slants, 10 ft depth, 8 ft height, 4 ft lower height, 16 ft bottom]

_____

UNIT 4 LESSON 3   Surface Area of Prisms **91**

4-3 Remembering

Solve.

1. At Pet Foods, dog food costs $10 for 5 pounds. At Buydogfood.com, the dog food costs $9 for 3 pounds. At which store is the food less expensive?

   _____

   _____

Name the prism.

2. 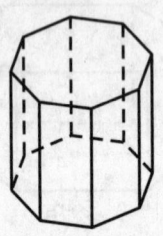 _____
3. 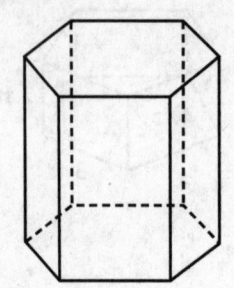 _____
4. _____

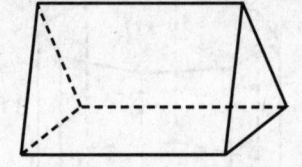

5. The perimeter of the base of a pentagonal prism is 45 cm. What is the width of the rectangular side of that prism?

   _____

6. The area of the base of a triangular prism is 60 ft², The height of the prism is 3 ft. If the widths of the rectangular faces are 8 ft, 15 ft, and 17 ft, what is the surface area of the triangular prism?

   _____

7. **Stretch Your Thinking** Jerome has a block of craft foam shaped like a square prism. He cuts the foam block in half. Jerome thinks that because the surface area of the original block was 358 in.², the surface area of each piece is 179 in.² Is he correct? Explain.

   _____

   _____

4-4 Homework

These nets form pyramids.
Use the shape of the base to name the pyramid.

1. _____

2. _____

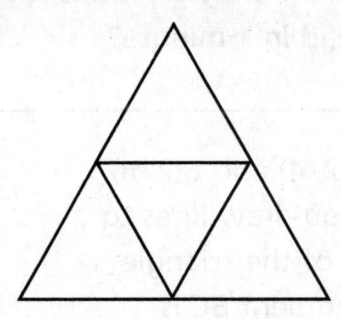

3. _____

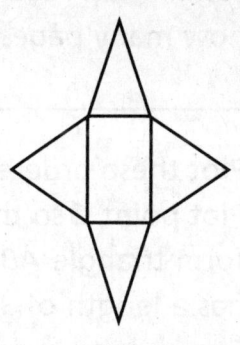

4. _____

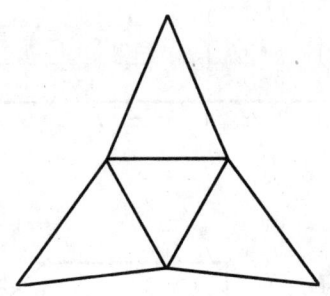

5. _____

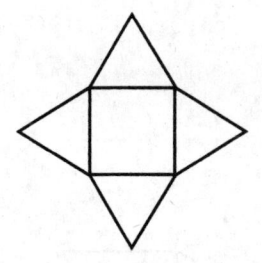

6. _____

Complete.

7. Will this net form a triangular pyramid? Explain.
_____

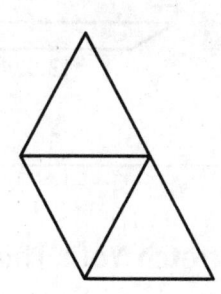

8. The perimeter of the base of a hexagonal pyramid is 48 in. The base is a regular polygon. What is the length of the base of one of the triangular faces?
_____

9. Vinnie found the area of a triangle with a base of 5 in. and a height of 6 in. to be 30 in.² What error did he make?
_____

10. Explain how you know how many triangular faces any pyramid will have?
_____
_____

UNIT 4 LESSON 4 — Nets for Pyramids 93

4-4 Remembering

Solve.

1. Sammy can read 20 pages in 5 minutes. At this rate, how many pages can she read in 1 minute?

   _____

2. Plot these ordered pairs: A(2, 4) and B(2, 8). Plot point C so that when you draw lines to form triangle ABC the base of the triangle has a length of 3 units. If segment BC is 5 units long, what is the perimeter and area of triangle ABC?

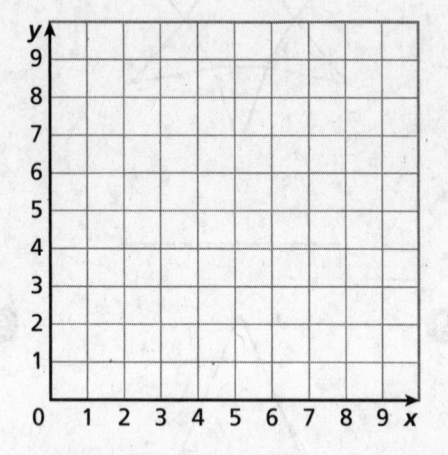

   P = _____

   A = _____

Find the surface area.

3. 4 yd, 6 yd, 13.5 yd

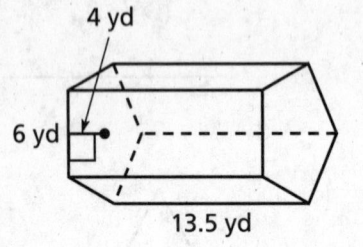

   _____

4. 11 in., 6 in., 7 in.

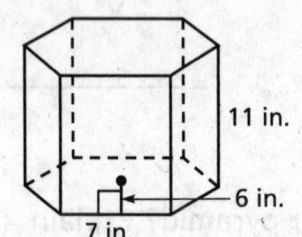

   _____

5. 5 cm, 6 cm, 8 cm

   _____

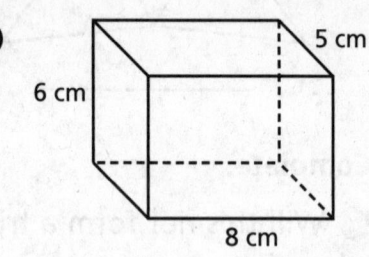

6. **Stretch Your Thinking** Marian glued together the wooden blocks as shown. Then she painted the faces of the blocks. How many square inches of paint did she use? Explain how you found your answer.

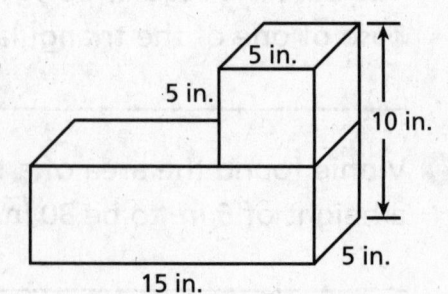

   (5 in., 5 in., 10 in., 5 in., 15 in.)

   _____

   _____

   _____

   _____

94 UNIT 4 LESSON 4 — Nets for Pyramids

4-5 Homework

Find the surface area. The bases of the pyramids in Exercises 1, 3, 4, 5, and 6 are regular polygons.

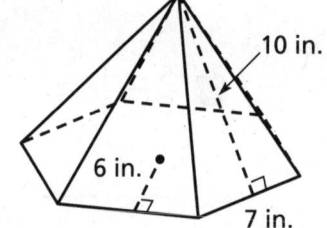

1. (square pyramid: slant height 11 ft, base edge 8 ft, apothem 8 ft shown)

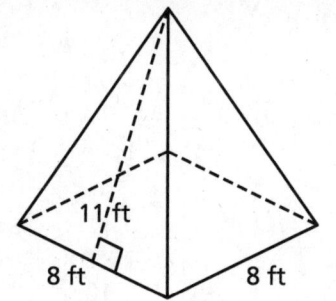

2. (rectangular pyramid: 30 m × 14 m base, slant heights 24 m and 20 m)

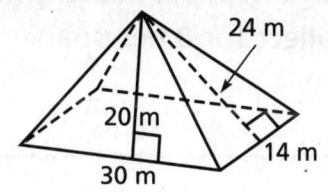

3. (triangular pyramid: slant height 14 m, base edge 12 m, apothem 10 m)

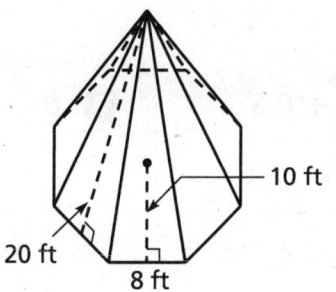

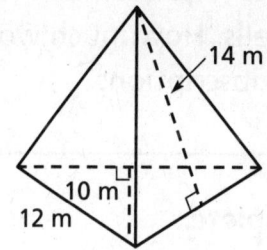

4. (hexagonal pyramid: slant height 10 in., apothem 6 in., base edge 7 in.)

5. (octagonal pyramid: slant height 20 ft, apothem 10 ft, base edge 8 ft)

6. (pentagonal pyramid: slant height 12 cm, apothem 7 cm, base edge 10 cm)

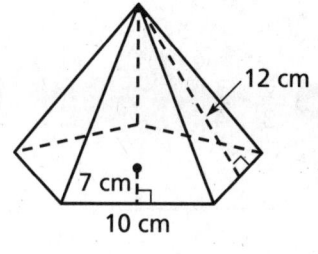

Solve.

7. The surface area of a square pyramid is 112 ft². If the length of each edge of the base is 8 ft., what is the slant height of each triangular face?

_____

8. The roof of this doghouse is a square pyramid. Each triangular face is 3 ft. high. If Jamal paints the roof and the sides, including the door, how much area will he paint?

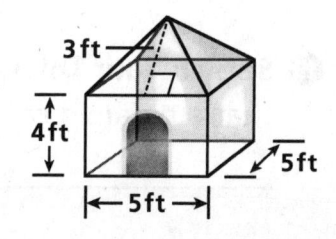

(doghouse: 5 ft × 5 ft base, 4 ft walls, 3 ft slant height on roof)

UNIT 4 LESSON 5 — Surface Area of Pyramids 95

4-5 Remembering

Solve.

1. Barry collects $24 for every 6 newspaper subscriptions he sells. How much would he collect for 8 newspaper subscriptions?
   _____

Complete.

2. 56×1.2

3. $456 + 443$

4. $2{,}334 - 976$

5. $\dfrac{10}{11} + \dfrac{1}{2}$

6. $\dfrac{2}{3} \cdot \dfrac{3}{4}$

7. $34.5 \div 0.5$

8. $\dfrac{2}{5} \div 1\dfrac{1}{5}$

9. $\dfrac{5}{6} - \dfrac{1}{3}$

Name the shape of the base and use it to name the pyramid.

10.

11.

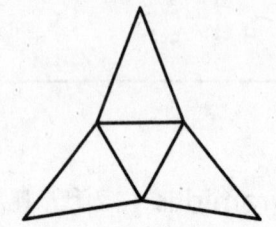

12.

13. **Stretch Your Thinking** What is the least number of faces that a pyramid can have? Explain.

_____

_____

_____

_____

Surface Area of Pyramids

4-6 Homework

Gina wants to make a pyramid container to hold popcorn.

1 Sketch below a small net for a pyramid container that will hold popcorn. Label the net with the actual dimensions you would like your container to have.

2 Use your net to find the surface area of your popcorn pyramid container.

UNIT 4 LESSON 6

4-6 Remembering

Solve.

1. Mr. O'Neil can buy a box of 8 pens for $24 at the ABC store. He can buy a box of 6 pens for $12 at the XYZ store. Mr. O'Neil wants to buy the pens for the lowest possible price. At which store should he buy the pens?

   _____

   _____

Name the pyramid. Then find the surface area.

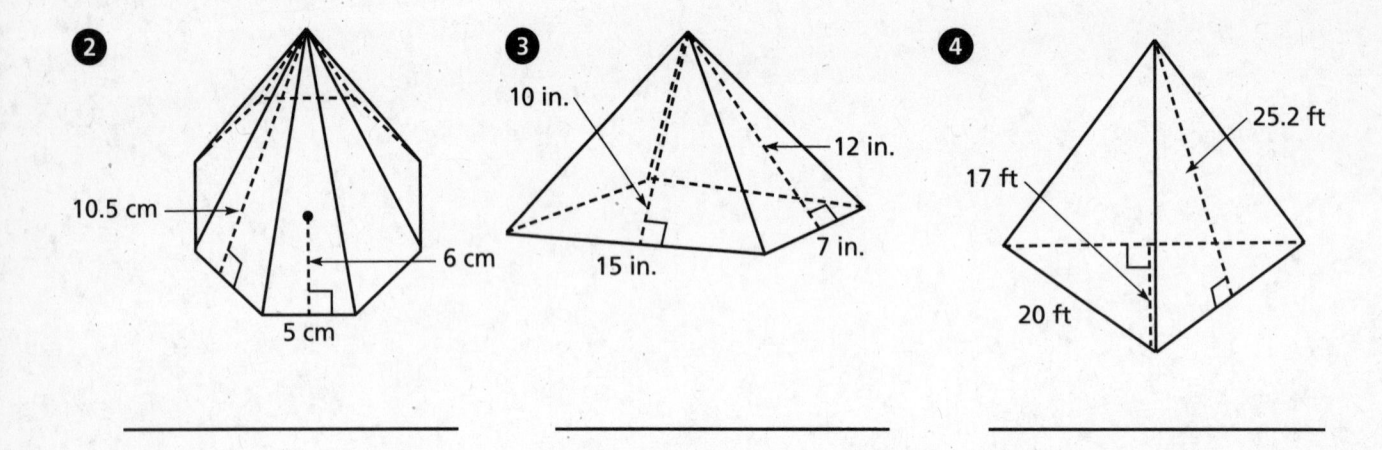

2. [Pyramid with 10.5 cm slant, 6 cm, 5 cm dimensions]

   _____

3. [Pyramid with 10 in., 12 in., 15 in., 7 in. dimensions]

   _____

4. [Pyramid with 25.2 ft, 17 ft, 20 ft dimensions]

   _____

5. **Stretch Your Thinking** Millie made the marble sculpture shown. She will treat the outside faces of the sculpture with marble protectant. How many square inches of the sculpture need to be treated? Explain how you found your answer.

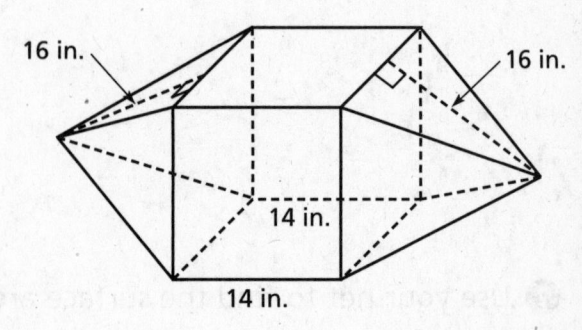

   [Sculpture with 16 in., 16 in., 14 in., 14 in. dimensions]

   _____

   _____

   _____

98 UNIT 4 LESSON 6 — Focus on Mathematical Practices